A CONCISE HISTORY OF SCOTLAND

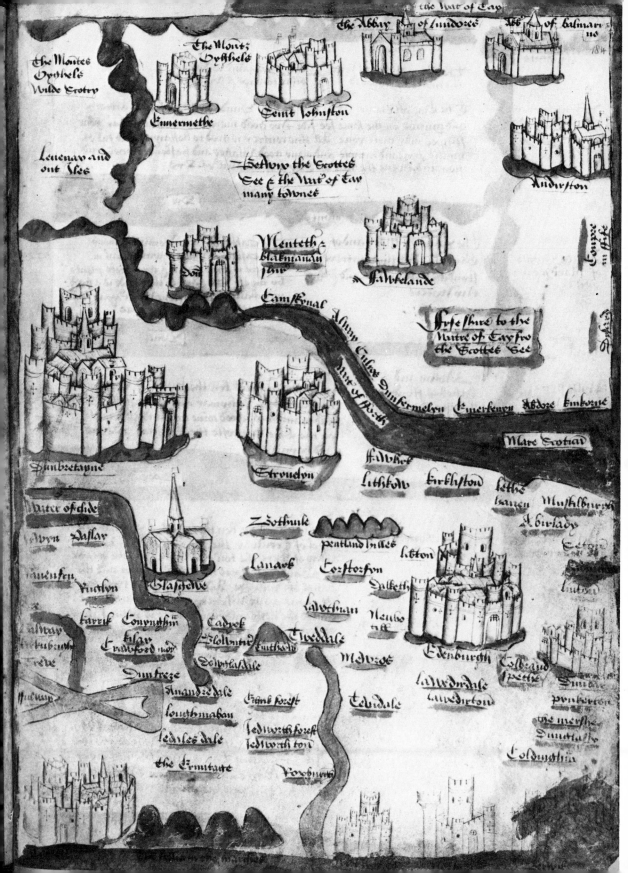

the Mut of Tay

the Abbay of Lundores

Abb of Balmari no

184

the Montz Gyskelz

the Montz Gyskelz Wilde Scotty

Seint Johnston

Enuermethe

Leuenax and out Iles

Betuix the Scottes See & the Mut of Tay many townes

Andirston

Menteth Blakmanni shir

Fouper in Fife

Falkelande

Camskynal Abnay Culros Dunfermelyn Emerkeny Abdore Kinhorne

Firste shire to the Mute of Tay fro the Scottes See

Dunbretayne

Frithe of Forth

Mare Scotici

Struelyn

Falkek

Litthkow

Kirkliston

Lettie baruy

Musklburgh

Vter of clide

Aberlady

Celyn Pasfar

Sottmuk

Seton

Peatland Inkes

rauenfen

Kinclyn

Glasshe

Lanark

Litton

Dalketh

Neubo tik

Edenburgh

Coldand spectie

calway bubant teue

farrik

Conynghm kilar Cradisford mor

Cadiot Blottmir Douglasdale

Tuedale

Mauore

Lawedrdale Lauedirton

pynkerton the mershe

Dunreze

Anandredale

Cutheow

Dunstafle

calway

louthmaban

Frank forist

Tebidale

Coldingham

Ieddes dale

Iedworth forist Iedwoth ton

the Ermitage

Roxburgh

A CONCISE HISTORY OF

SCOTLAND

FITZROY MACLEAN

with 231 illustrations

Here's tae us –
Wha's like us?
SCOTTISH SAYING

BEEKMAN HOUSE · NEW YORK

ACKNOWLEDGMENTS

My thanks are due to Lady Hesketh, Lady Antonia Fraser, Miss Janet Glover and Sir Iain Moncreiffe of that Ilk for their invaluable comments and criticism; also to Mr John Colville, C.B., C.V.O., for the additional verse of the National Anthem quoted on page 173; and finally to Miss Priscilla Thorburn for her invaluable help in preparing the text for publication.

Frontispiece: 'From the Border to the Tay'.
Detail of a map of Scotland, *c.* 1460

Contents

1 'POLISHED FROM THE RUST
   OF SCOTTISH BARBARITY'   *page 9*

> The mists of antiquity / the Romans / four races / the coming of Christian-
> ity / Columba / the Norsemen / Malcolm Ceann Mor / the Normans / the
> French Alliance / the Maid of Norway / the Succession / Edward I of
> England

2 'NOT FOR GLORY, NOR RICHES, NOR HONOUR,
   BUT ONLY FOR THAT LIBERTY'   *page 37*

> William Wallace / Robert Bruce / Bannockburn / the House of Stewart /
> the great nobles / the Kingdom of the Isles / the Red Harlaw

3 'THEY SPEND ALL THEIR TIME IN WARS AND WHEN
   THERE IS NO WAR THEY FIGHT ONE ANOTHER' *page 63*

> James IV / the Renaissance / the Highland Clans / the Auld Alliance /
> Flodden Field / brawling nobles / the Rough Wooing / the coming of the
> Reformation / John Knox / Mary Queen of Scots / her abdication

4 'THE GREAT MARRIAGE DAY
   OF THIS NATION WITH GOD'   *page 101*

> A succession of Regents / James VI and the Kirk / 'No Bishops, no King' /
> the Union of the Crowns / the rise of Clan Campbell / Charles I / the
> National Covenant / Montrose / Cromwell

5 'ANE END OF ANE AULD SANG'   *page 133*

> The Commonwealth / the Restoration / Charles II / the Covenanters /
> the Killing Time / James VII / William and Mary / Killiecrankie /
> Glencoe / *Mi-run mor nan Gall* / Darien / the Union

6 'THE KING OVER THE WATER'   *page 157*

> The Fifteen / Old Mr Melancholy / the Nineteen / the Forty-Five / Charlie's
> Year

7 'FOR A' THAT'   *page 181*

> 'Lochaber no more' / 'The more the mischief the better the sport' / the
> Crown as link / Industrial Revolution / political stagnation / a flowering
> of the arts / return of confidence / the Empire / the established Church /
> the Reform Bill / the shifting balance of the parties / more devolution /
> the Scottish economy / union or separation?

GENEALOGY OF THE SCOTTISH KINGS   *page 219*

LIST OF ILLUSTRATIONS   *page 221*

INDEX   *page 233*

For Veronica

Chapter One

'POLISHED FROM THE RUST
OF SCOTTISH BARBARITY'

The early history of Scotland, like that of most countries, is largely veiled by what are known as the mists of antiquity, in this case a more than usually felicitous phrase. From piles of discarded sea-shells and implements of bone and stone, from monoliths and megaliths and mounds of grass-grown turf, from *crannogs* and *brochs* and vitrified forts, painstaking archaeologists have pieced together a handful of basic facts about the Stone and Bronze Age inhabitants of our country and about the first Celtic invaders who followed them in successive waves a good many centuries later. But it is not until the beginning of our own era that we come upon the first written records of Scottish history. These are to

Prehistoric standing stones of Stenness, Orkney.

Skara Brae, Orkney: Stone Age dwelling place.

be found in the works of the Roman historian Tacitus, whose father-in-law, Cnaeus Julius Agricola, then Governor of the Roman Province of Britain, invaded what is now southern Scotland with the Ninth Legion in the year AD 81.

From Tacitus we learn that, having advanced from a base in northern England as far as the Forth–Clyde line, which it was his intention to hold by means of a chain of forts, Agricola established his headquarters at Stirling. Keeping in touch with his fleet as he pushed northwards, he encountered and heavily defeated the native Caledonians under their chieftain Calgacus in a pitched battle at Mons Graupius in eastern Scotland, which some identify as the Hill of Moncreiffe.

This was in the late summer of 83. After wintering on the banks of the Tay, Agricola was proposing to continue his advance northwards when early in 84 he suddenly received orders from Rome to withdraw. '*Perdomita Britannia et*

Hadrian, Emperor of Rome AD 117–38, whose head is shown (*left*) on a gold coin, visited Britain in 121, and ordered the building of a defensive wall against the raiding northern tribes. This wall, from Solway to Tyne, still stands for most of its length.

Opposite: view from Cuddy's Crag.

statim omissa', wrote Tacitus sourly, 'Britain conquered and then at once thrown away.' Subsequent Roman strategy towards Scotland seems to have been mainly defensive rather than offensive in intention. In 121 the Emperor Hadrian himself visited Britain and built his wall from Solway to Tyne. And twenty years after this we find the then Governor of Britain, Lollius Urbicus, building in his turn the Antonine Wall from Forth to Clyde.

Later again, in 208, the old Emperor Severus, no doubt encouraged by the series of spectacular victories he had won from Illyria to the Euphrates, tried a new approach to the problem, building himself a naval base at Cramond and then pushing northwards as far as the Moray Firth. But his Caledonian adversaries, wiser than their forefathers, avoided a pitched battle, and after three years of inconclusive skirmishing old Severus was back at Eboracum or York, dying from his exertions.

The tangled mountain mass of the Grampians and the dense forest which at that time covered much of central Scotland favoured guerrilla warfare and the

Roman cavalryman riding down four northern tribesmen. Carved stone slab from the Antonine Wall, 2nd century A D.

Caledonians took full advantage of them. Not long after Severus' campaign the Romans abandoned the Antonine Wall and evacuated their northerly bases. For a hundred years or more Hadrian's Wall remained the Roman frontier and Britain to the south of it enjoyed a period of relative peace. Then, in the second half of the fourth century the tribes began to break through from the north in a series of ever bolder and more successful raids. At the same time Saxon pirates started to attack from across the North Sea. Had the Romans not had their hands full elsewhere, they might have returned to their original project of trying to conquer Scotland. As it was, trouble nearer home made it necessary for the Legions to be recalled and by the end of the fourth century the last remaining Roman outposts in Scotland had been abandoned. Thus Scotland only encountered the might of Rome spasmodically and never became a true part of the Roman Empire or enjoyed save at second hand the benefits or otherwise of Roman civilization.

Part of a hoard of 4th-century Roman silver plate found at Traprain Law, East Lothian. *Above:* flagon, decorated with Biblical scenes; *left:* two silver chalices; *left, below:* silver bowl with a frieze of hunting motifs – hyenas attacking sheep.

13

The Picts, of Celtic stock, are thought to have reached Scotland from the Continent some time during the first millennium B C. This elaborate jet necklace, found at Poltalloch, Argyll, dates to the very earliest period of this migration.

By about 430 the Romans had also evacuated Britain south of Hadrian's Wall, leaving the inhabitants to their own devices and to the mercy of their more warlike and less civilized neighbours. Soon barbaric Teuton invaders from across the North Sea, the Angles and Saxons, had taken over most of what is now England, driving the native Britons westwards into Wales and Cornwall and northwards into Cumbria and Strathclyde.

Picts and Scots

Scotland was at this time divided between four different races. Of these the most powerful were the Picts, who were supreme from Caithness in the north to the Forth in the south. Of Celtic stock, they had, according to some authorities, originally arrived from the continent of Europe as part of the Celtic migrations which reached the British Isles at different times during the first millennium before Christ. Some said they were of Scythian origin.

The neighbouring Britons of Strathclyde, another Celtic race, speaking a kindred tongue, controlled the area stretching from the Clyde to the Solway and beyond into Cumbria. To the east, the country south of the Forth was now occupied by the Teutonic Anglo-Saxons who held sway over an area stretching southwards into Northumbria. Like their Anglo-Saxon kinsmen further south, they came from the lands lying between the mouth of the Rhine and the Baltic.

An incised relief on an Orkney gravestone shows three Pictish warriors, strangely Assyrian in their stance.

14

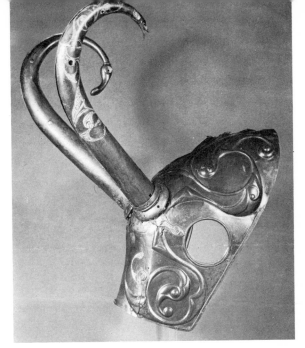

A carved sandstone slab from Ross-shire (*left*) shows a hunting scene with a horsewoman and two trumpeters. The sophisticated style of decoration suggests a date of about A D 800. *Above:* Chamfrain of engraved and beaten bronze, perhaps as early as 200 B C. This strange piece of armour protected the faces of horses that drew the war chariots of Celtic chieftains.

Finally, to the west, embracing what is now Argyll, Kintyre and the neighbouring islands, lay the Kingdom of Dalriada. This had been colonized in the third and fourth centuries of our era by the Scots, a warlike Celtic race from Northern Ireland, who, though at first overshadowed by the Picts, were eventually to give their name to all Scotland, which at this time was still known as Alba or Alban. Although Picts and Scots periodically combined to harass the Romans, the Scots, who spoke a different Celtic language and whose first loyalties were to their fellow Scots across the sea in Irish Dalriada, had from the start been in conflict with their Pictish neighbours. It was a conflict that was to take much bloodshed and several hundred years to resolve.

In the course of the three centuries that followed the departure of the Romans, the Picts, the Scots, the Britons and finally even the Angles were all, nominally at any rate, converted to Christianity. The task that confronted the early Christian missionaries was not an easy one. Pagan prejudices and traditions were deeply rooted; the tribes they went among were warlike and at odds with each

Christian Missionaries

other; the country was mountainous and wild. But the age was one that threw up a whole sequence of men remarkable for their toughness, their strength of character and their devotion to their faith.

There are indications that already in Roman days little Christian communities existed north of Hadrian's Wall. There were no doubt Christians amongst the legionaries and from them the new faith spread to the native population. 'Places among the Britons unpenetrated by the Romans have come under the rule of Christ,' wrote Tertullian in 208, '*Britannorum inaccessa Romanis loca, Christo vero subdita.*' St Ninian, the first of the great Christian missionaries to Alban, was himself the son of Christian parents. After visiting Rome and being consecrated a bishop there, he returned in 397 or 398 to his native Strathclyde and there established a monastery, known as Candida Casa, at Whithorn near the Solway. This was soon to serve as a seminary and starting point for Christian missions, not only to the Britons, but also to the Picts. But, though St Ninian's missionaries pushed northwards up the Great Glen towards Caithness and Sutherland and, according to some accounts, even reached the Orkneys and Shetland, they seem, partly no doubt for linguistic reasons and partly for reasons of geography, to have had but little contact with Dalriada.

The Papil Stone, from Shetland (Pictish, early 9th century): the bird-men typify Pictish obsession with myths and monsters.

Entangled animal figures and interlocking spirals on this Pictish cross-slab (*left*) of the 8th century recall the style of the roughly contemporary Lindisfarne Gospels.

St Ninian, first of the great Christian missionaries to Scotland, is shown (*opposite*) in a 15th-century book of hours, robed as a bishop.

16

St Columba, missionary and statesman, came from Ireland to Iona in 563. Pen drawing from a 9th-century Life by Adamnan.

Through the centuries, the first Scottish settlers in Dalriada, while consolidating their hold on the territories they had conquered, had remained in close touch with their parent kingdom in Ireland. Then in about the year 500, Fergus MacErc and his two brothers, Angus and Lorne, led a fresh Scottish invasion from Ireland and established a new dynasty with its stronghold at Dunadd near Crinan, which now became the capital of Scottish Dalriada. But Fergus and his successors continued to pay tribute to Ireland and to accept Irish suzerainty and it was from Ireland that towards the middle of the sixth

On the site of St Columba's monastery, and of a later medieval abbey, stands the recently rebuilt Iona Cathedral. In the foreground, St Martin's Cross (*see opposite*).

century the first Christian missionaries reached Dalriada. The earliest of these was St Oran, who died of the plague in 548, after establishing Christian churches in Iona, Mull and Tiree, though not as yet on the mainland. Then in 563 St Columba arrived from Ireland and, having established himself on Iona, at once made it a base for his missions to the mainland and to the other islands.

Columba was by any standards a remarkable man. Of royal birth and powerful intellect and physique, he seems to have left Ireland under some kind of a cloud. In Scottish Dalriada his impact was to a high degree political as well as spiritual. Arriving on the scene at a moment when the Scots had suffered a crushing military defeat at the hands of the Picts, when their king had been killed, their morale was low and their very independence was threatened, he not only preached the Gospel, but at once took active measures to re-establish and consolidate the monarchy. Aidan the False, whom he now made king in place of the rightful heir to the throne, proved an astute and resourceful monarch. The good work which he began was carried on by his descendants, especially Eochaid the Venomous, who successfully infiltrated the enemy camp by marrying a Pictish princess. It was not long before the Scots were once again more than holding their own against the Picts.

From Dalriada, Columba penetrated far into northern Pictland, quelling a monster which he encountered in Loch Ness and easily getting the best of the pagan priests he found at the court of the local king. By his death in 579 Dunadd had become an established political capital, while Iona was the nucleus of a

St Martin's Cross, Iona.

The Temptation of Christ: illumination from the Book of Kells. This superb 9th-century manuscript, now in Dublin, may have been started in the Monastery of Iona.

19

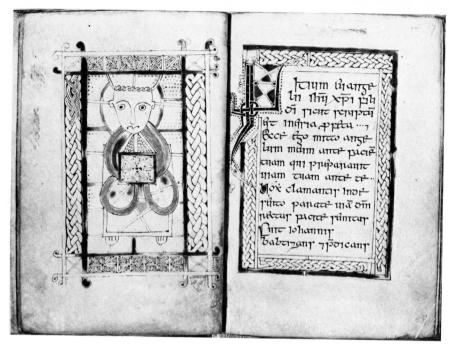

Beginning of the Gospel of St Mark, in Latin, with a representation of the Evangelist. From the 9th-century Book of Deer.

fast-expanding Church, organized, it may be observed, on lines that were not as yet episcopal.

From Ireland, too, came St Moluag, who founded a monastery in 562 on the Island of Lismore, and St Maelrubba, who established himself at Applecross a century later. From the west both travelled up and down Dalriada and far into Pictish territory, founding missions and monasteries as they went. Soon after St Columba's death St Aidan had gone out from Iona to convert the Angles of Northumbria, establishing himself on Holy Island near Bamburgh, while St Cuthbert, the apostle of the Anglo-Saxon Lothians, likewise drew his inspiration from the same source.

Though by the end of the seventh century all four of the kingdoms of Alban had been converted to Christianity, they were still far from being united among themselves politically. Nor were they in unison theologically with the rest of Christendom. Out of touch with Rome, the Celtic clergy had developed views on such subjects as the style of the tonsure and the date of Easter which struck the Vatican and their fellow Christians further south as deplorable. 'Wicked', 'lewd' and 'wrongful', were some of the phrases used in this connection by no less an authority than the Venerable Bede. In the end the Celts were to yield

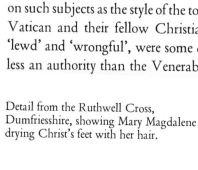

Detail from the Ruthwell Cross, Dumfriesshire, showing Mary Magdalene drying Christ's feet with her hair.

before superior wealth and organization. But they had made a notable contribution to the Christian heritage. 'The Celtic Church gave love', ran the saying, 'the Roman Church gave law.' It was the law that in the end prevailed.

Trouble, meanwhile, threatened from another quarter. From the end of the eighth century onwards the Norsemen began their attacks on Scotland, gradually gaining a foothold, and then more than a foothold, on the islands and coastal areas. By the end of the ninth century, they had conquered Orkney, Shetland and the Western Isles and these were followed by Caithness and Sutherland.

The divisions and disagreements of the four kingdoms weakened their resistance to the common enemy. Hostility still persisted between Picts and Scots, while the Britons of Strathclyde would have no truck with the Angles of Lothian and Northumbria. For a time it had seemed possible that the Angles would achieve ascendancy over their neighbours, but the decisive defeat of their King Ecgfrith by the Picts at the battle of Nectansmere in 685 effectively ruled this out.

It was not until the ninth century that some measure of unity was at last achieved. In the year 843 Kenneth MacAlpin, King of the Scots of Dalriada and at the same time a claimant to the Pictish throne, a man, we are told, 'of marvellous astuteness', fell upon the Picts, to whose ruling dynasty he was related, after they had been weakened by the raids of the Norsemen, and, having disposed of all rival claimants, made himself King of everything north of the Forth. From Dunadd he moved his capital to Forteviot in the heart of

Kenneth MacAlpin

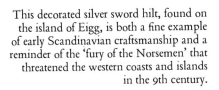
This decorated silver sword hilt, found on the island of Eigg, is both a fine example of early Scandinavian craftsmanship and a reminder of the 'fury of the Norsemen' that threatened the western coasts and islands in the 9th century.

The Monymusk Reliquary (*left*), in which the remains of St Columba were taken by King Kenneth MacAlpin from Iona to Dunkeld. The Hunterston Brooch (*right*) is a typical piece of Celtic 8th-century craftsmanship, in silver-gilt, set with amber.

Pictish territory while the religious centre of his kingdom was shifted to Dunkeld. Thither he now transferred St Columba's remains from Iona. 'And so', says the Huntingdon Chronicle, 'he was the first of the Scots to obtain the monarchy of the whole of Albania, which is now called Scotia.'

Of the Picts, who had ruled over most of Scotland for more than a thousand years, little or nothing more was heard. They were, in the modern phrase, *gleichgeschaltet* and so have gone down to history as a shadowy, ill-documented race of people of uncertain antecedents, possibly tattooed or 'painted', for that, after all, is the Latin meaning of their name.*

Right up to his death in 858, Kenneth MacAlpin sought repeatedly to conquer the Angles of Lothian. But in this he was unsuccessful. His successors, involved as they were in continuous warfare with the Norsemen, fared no better, and it was not until more than a century and a half later, in 1018, that his descendant Malcolm II's victory over the Angles at Carham finally brought the Lothians under Scottish rule. In the same year the King of the Britons of Strathclyde died without issue and was succeeded by Malcolm's grandson and heir Duncan, who had managed to establish some kind of claim to the throne of

* With all due respect to W. C. Mackenzie, who dismisses it as 'an interpretation that leads nowhere'.

Strathclyde through the female line. Sixteen years later, in 1034, Duncan succeeded his grandfather as King of Scotland. In this way the frontiers of the Scottish kingdom were still further extended, reaching far down into what is now English territory.

In 1040, after a short, rather unhappy reign, Duncan was killed in battle by Maelbeatha or Macbeth, the Mormaer of Moray, who claimed the throne both on his own behalf and on that of his wife, and now made himself king in Duncan's place. Macbeth appears, contrary to popular belief, to have been a wise monarch and to have ruled Scotland successfully and well for seventeen prosperous years. In 1050 we hear that he went on a pilgrimage to Rome and there 'scattered money among the poor like seed'. But seven years later he was defeated and killed by Duncan's elder son, Malcolm, who thus regained for his family his father's throne to which he had never abandoned his claim.

Malcolm III, known to his contemporaries as Ceann Mor or Bighead, had been brought up in England from the age of nine. In 1069, twelve years after his return to Scotland, he married, as his second wife, the English Princess Margaret, who had taken refuge in Scotland with her brother Edgar the Atheling after the Norman Conquest of England in 1066.

Malcolm and Margaret

Part of a set of chessmen carved from walrus ivory (Scandinavian, 12th century), found on the island of Lewis in 1831. The king (*right*) is about four inches high.

St Margaret, Queen of Malcolm III Ceann Mor (from a 15th-century illumination). Under her influence and Malcolm's, Court life became more civilized, and English fashions and customs were introduced. She ordered the rebuilding of the Monastery of Iona and for her benefactions to the Church she was canonized in 1251.

The Norman Conquest was to prove almost as important for Scotland as it was for England. Henceforth England and her rulers were in one way or another to play an ever greater part in Scottish affairs. English and Norman influences were to make themselves increasingly felt in the Lowlands, while under Malcolm and his successors the foundations of feudalism were laid, at any rate in southern Scotland. Margaret, a saintly and determined young woman, set herself to introduce at her husband's Court English fashions and English customs. She also took the Scottish clergy in hand and, to their dismay, sought to impose on them the religious practices prevalent in England, celibacy, poverty, and so on. Soon, under her guidance, life at Court assumed a more civilized tinge, while in the Church a system of regular diocesan episcopacy gradually began to take shape. Malcolm, being himself English-educated, was inclined to share his wife's views and during his reign shifted the cultural centre of his kingdom southwards into Anglo-Saxon Lothian, thereby seriously offending the Celtic North.

But Malcolm's interest in his southern neighbour was strategic as well as cultural. The northern counties of England seemed to him to offer possibilities for expansion and in his brother-in-law Edgar the Atheling he had at his Court a ready-made claimant to the English throne. He accordingly launched a series of border-raids into Northumberland and Cumberland. These provoked retaliatory expeditions on the part of the Normans and in 1071 William the Conqueror finally invaded Scotland and forced Malcolm to pay homage to him at Abernethy. In the intervals of the fighting amicable relations were maintained between the two countries, for Malcolm had remained a popular figure at the English Court. In 1093, however, in the course of an attack on Alnwick in Northumberland (intended, it was said, to forestall a Norman invasion), he was killed in an ambush by one of his Norman friends named Morel. Queen Margaret, for her part, died three days later, piously uttering a prayer of thanks that such sadness should have been sent to purify her last moments. She was in due course canonized.

For thirty years after Malcolm's death, Scotland was in turmoil, ruled over by a succession of weak, insecure kings. The first of these was Malcolm's sixty-year-old brother, Donald Ban, who after his father's death, while Malcolm was in England, had been sent off to the Hebrides. He had thus fallen under Norse and Celtic rather than English or Norman influence and on his brother's death, having seized the throne, at once reversed Malcolm's Anglo-Norman attitudes and policies.

At Abernethy in Perthshire is one of the three remaining ancient round towers in Scotland; they were built by Celtic monks as a defence against marauding Vikings. It was at Abernethy that Malcolm was forced to pay homage to William I in 1071.

The earliest extant Scottish charter records a gift of land by Duncan II to the Abbey of St Cuthbert, Durham.

This did not endear the new king to William Rufus, who had succeeded to the English throne on the death of his father, William the Conqueror. In 1094 he sent Duncan, Malcolm's son by his first marriage, whom he had been holding in England as a hostage, to dethrone his uncle by force. Duncan succeeded in this. He was, however, almost immediately murdered and old Donald Ban restored to the throne. But not for long. In 1097 an Anglo-Norman force chased Donald out again and made Duncan's half-brother Edgar king in his place. Edgar believed in helping those who helped him, and during his reign more Normans than ever were settled in southern Scotland. He came to terms, too, with Magnus Barelegs, the King of Norway, formally ceding to him the Hebrides and Kintyre, of which the Norwegians had in fact long been in possession. Thus St Columba's sanctuary of Iona, for so long the burial-place of the Scottish kings, became Norse territory and old Donald Ban was the last of his dynasty to be buried there.

On Edgar's death in 1107 he was succeeded by yet another brother, Alexander, like him the son of Malcolm and Margaret. Alexander, however, only ruled over the land between Forth and Spey, leaving Argyll, Ross and even Moray to their own devices, while responsibility for Scotland south of the Forth was entrusted to his younger brother David. Alexander's sister Maud had become the wife of King Henry I of England, while he himself had married Henry's beautiful, luxury-loving natural daughter Sibylla. He was thus at one and the same time Henry's brother-in-law and son-in-law and in his reign the con-

Tomb of the Kings, Iona, traditionally the burial-place of the three founders of Dalriada. Here all the Scottish kings were buried until Iona was ceded to King Magnus Barelegs of Norway in 1098. The tomb slabs shown here are those of chiefs and bishops buried later, over the kings.

26

On a sarcophagus at St Andrews, probably the shrine of St Regulus, founder of the church, King David I is represented symbolically as a shepherd, a hunter and a slayer of lions.

nection with England grew still closer and English and Norman influence greater than ever.

David I

In 1124 Alexander died and was succeeded by his brother David, the ninth son of Malcolm III and already the ruler of most of southern Scotland. David, by a long way the most remarkable of Malcolm and Margaret's children, was to rule Scotland for close on thirty years. They were to be eventful years for Scotland. Like his brothers, David had been brought up in England, where he had received a Norman education and made many Norman friends and where, we learn from the patronizing William of Malmesbury, his manners 'were polished from the rust of Scottish barbarity'. In addition to being King of Scotland, he was in his own right Prince of Cumbria, and, by his marriage to a rich Norman heiress, Earl of Northampton and Huntingdon. He was thus one of the most powerful barons in England as well as being the English King's brother-in-law.

On returning to Scotland, he proceeded to distribute large estates there amongst his Anglo-Norman friends and associates, such as de Brus, Walter fitzAlan, a Breton who became his High Steward, de Bailleul, de Comines and many others, who thus became landowners on both sides of the Border. The Church, too, became the preserve of Norman prelates. Simultaneously David introduced into the Lowlands of Scotland something more closely resembling a feudal system of ownership, founded on a new, French-speaking, Anglo-Norman aristocracy, who, although they intermarried and eventually merged with the old Celtic aristocracy, remained for a time separate and distinct from the

27

Opposite: Dryburgh Abbey, Berwickshire: doorway from the cloisters to the nave. Founded in 1150, it was granted a charter by David I.

David was the first Scottish king to issue his own autonomous coinage. Sterling silver coin, minted at Berwick.

native population, many of whom still spoke Gaelic, save in the south and east where they spoke a primitive form of English. In the Highlands, meanwhile, a different, more patriarchal system prevailed and the King's writ counted for very little, while the Islands and parts of the mainland gave a loose allegiance to Norway.

In the course of his reign David sought, in so far as he could, to establish a national system of justice and administration under his own over-all control. Alexander had already appointed a number of Court officials, such as Chamberlain, Constable, Chancellor, Steward and Marshal. From these and from the bishops David selected a central governing body to advise him, to carry out his commands and to deal with major administrative and judicial problems. He further appointed justiciars and sheriffs to administer justice. In the economic field he encouraged trade with foreign countries and established two royal mints and a standard system of weights and measures. He also granted the status of burgh to a number of towns, together with freedom from tolls, the right to hold markets and fairs and also monopolies in respect of certain products. In order to keep in touch with his subjects, though also on sanitary grounds, he and his advisers moved constantly about the country from one royal castle to another.

Being a devout man, David also turned his attention to ecclesiastical matters, founding more bishoprics (under Anglo-Norman bishops) at Glasgow, Brechin, Dunblane, Caithness, Ross and Aberdeen, establishing more parishes, building more churches and endowing more monasteries, among them Kelso, Dryburgh and Melrose. But, while he accepted in general the universal claims of Rome, David wished the Scottish Church to retain a certain autonomy. Though ordered by Pope Innocent III, under threat of excommunication, to acknowledge the supremacy of the Archbishop of York, the Scottish Bishops, with the King's encouragement, rejected this proposition out of hand and so started a dispute which was to drag on for the remainder of the century.

29

David I and his grandson, 'Malcolm the Maiden', who succeeded him at the age of eleven as Malcolm IV. Miniature from the Charter of Kelso Abbey, 1159.

David's long reign was for the most part peaceful. In 1135, however, he chose to intervene in the dynastic disputes which developed in England, on the death of King Henry I, between his daughter Maud and her cousin Stephen. These he turned to his own advantage, successfully playing one side off against the other and, though defeated in 1138 at the Battle of the Standard near Northallerton, emerged, thanks to skilful negotiation, with precisely what he wanted, namely the greater part of Northumbria.

When David came to the throne in 1124, Scotland had, even by the standards of the day, been a primitive country with practically no towns and scarcely any industry or commerce. People lived in wooden houses and such trade as existed was conducted by barter. The different parts of the country were cut off from each other by barren stretches of uninhabited moorland and hill. It could hardly even be said that there was a common language. Latin, French, English and a number of Gaelic dialects were all spoken in different areas and by different classes of the population. In the absence of any established feudal system, local chieftains felt free to disregard the authority of the King and of the central government. The Church, with only three bishops and no properly organized system of parishes, had very little influence one way or the other. When David died in 1153 much had changed. In the Lowlands, at any rate, what remained of the old Celtic way of life had been swept away and a new, relatively efficient, Anglo-Norman order of things established in its place.

On David's death, the throne passed to his eldest grandson, Malcolm IV, a boy of eleven, known to history as the Maiden. At once, the King of Norway

Coin of William I, known as 'the Lion'. It was William the Lion who concluded the alliance with France that came to be known as the 'Auld Alliance'.

sacked Aberdeen; there was unrest in Moray, while Somerled, Lord of Argyll, sailed up the Clyde and sacked Glasgow. King Henry II Plantagenet, who had finally come to the English throne in 1154, seized the opportunity to send for little Malcolm and force him to return Northumbria to England.

Malcolm did not live long. On his death in 1165 he was succeeded by his more enterprising brother William the Lion. Resenting the loss of Northumbria, William, after first concluding in 1165 a formal alliance with France, to be known to succeeding generations as the Auld Alliance, launched in 1174 a grand invasion of England at a moment when he had reason to hope that Henry II's attention was engaged elsewhere. But the enterprise misfired. Thanks to their own rashness and to an East Coast mist, attributed by both sides to divine intervention, the Scots were heavily defeated at Alnwick and William himself taken prisoner and sent by the English to Normandy. There he was forced to sign the Treaty of Falaise. By this humiliating document Scotland was placed under feudal subjection to England, the Scottish Church put under the jurisdiction of the English Primate, Northumbria confirmed as English territory and the main castles of southern Scotland garrisoned by English troops.

The Auld Alliance

Fifteen years were to pass before William was able to redress the balance. In 1189 Richard Cœur de Lion of England, needing money for a crusade, agreed to hand back the castles occupied in 1174 and to renounce his feudal superiority over Scotland in return for 10,000 marks. Three years later, Pope Celestine III released the Scottish Church from English supremacy and decreed that thenceforth it should be under the direct jurisdiction of Rome. It was the

31

beginning of more than a hundred years of peace between Scotland and England.

The King and
the Chieftains

But the Scottish kings did not only have their English neighbours to contend with. The Celtic chieftains of the west, who still enjoyed a great measure of independence, were in a state of more or less permanent insurrection against the central monarchy. Fergus, Prince of Galloway, had rebelled no less than three times against Malcolm the Maiden before retiring to a monastery, and in the reign of William the Lion his sons rose again, massacring, with particular gusto, the Anglo-Norman garrisons which had been stationed in southern Scotland under the Treaty of Falaise. It was to be a long time before this last Celtic stronghold of the south-west was finally pacified.

Further north, in what is now Argyllshire, were the dominions of the Lords of Lorne and the Lords of the Isles. These regarded themselves with reason as independent rulers with no particular loyalty or obligations to the royal house of Scotland, their allegiance being rather to the kings of Norway. Already in the reign of Malcolm the Maiden, as we have seen, the part-Norse Somerled, King of Morvern, Lochaber, Argyll and the southern Hebrides and uncle by marriage to the Norwegian King of the Isles, had, as we have seen, shown his contempt for the Scottish kings by sailing up the Clyde and sacking Glasgow. An unlucky spear-thrust had laid him low and his followers had been beaten off by Malcolm's High Steward, Walter fitzAlan, Lord of Renfrew. But Somerled's descendants, the Macdougall Lords of Lorne and the Macdonald Lords of the Isles, were, in their turn, to carry on the tradition of independence.

When William the Lion died in 1214, he was succeeded by his son Alexander II, a capable ruler who put to good use the administrative machine created by David I. Alexander seems in his turn to have hankered after Northumbria, but in the end abandoned his claims and accepted a number of estates in northern England in settlement of the dispute. He was now free to turn to his own domestic problems. In his reign, as in those of his predecessors, there were insurrections in Galloway, Argyll, Moray and Caithness, and when he died in 1249, he was on his way to attempt the conquest of the Western Isles whose Lords still chose to give their allegiance to the kings of Norway.

This task, interrupted by his death, was resumed by his son Alexander III who, when scarcely more than a boy, launched his first raids against the Hebrides. Disturbed at these encroachments on his domains, old King Hakon of Norway decided to retaliate and in the summer of 1263 assembled a great fleet with which he sailed for Scotland. By opening negotiations with the

Sterling silver coin
of Alexander II,
minted at Berwick.

Norwegians, Alexander managed to delay giving battle until October. This was the season of autumn gales and these, as he had hoped, played havoc with Hakon's fleet as it lay in the Firth of Clyde. In the end the Norwegians fought their way ashore at Largs in Ayrshire, where, in the course of a rather confused engagement, they were defeated on land as well as at sea and withdrew in disorder. Old Hakon himself died at Kirkwall on his way home to Norway and his successor Magnus signed a peace under which the Hebrides now became part of Scotland, though remaining in practice an independent kingdom under the Lords of the Isles, who for their part paid no more heed to their Scottish than they had to their Norwegian overlords. Orkney and Shetland were left for the time being in Norwegian hands.

The remainder of Alexander's reign was both peaceful and prosperous. His marriage to Margaret, the daughter of the English King Henry III, secured peace with England, while in 1283 the marriage of their daughter Margaret to King Eric of Norway set the seal on the Peace Treaty of twenty years before between Scotland and Norway and established, after four centuries of strife, a friendly relationship between the two countries which has lasted ever since. Meanwhile, at home trade improved, the revenue increased, law and order were maintained, education, within its limits, prospered, more building was done, both domestic and ecclesiastical, and for most people life became less disagreeable than it had been.

Viking silver penny, *c.* 880, showing a longship.

Representation of a Viking ship on a Swedish runic stone, *c.* 800.

PARLIAMENT
of EDWARD I.

A Parliament of Edward I in 1274; to the King's right sits Alexander III of Scotland, to his left Llewellyn, Prince of Wales, and before them the 'lords spiritual and temporal'.

33

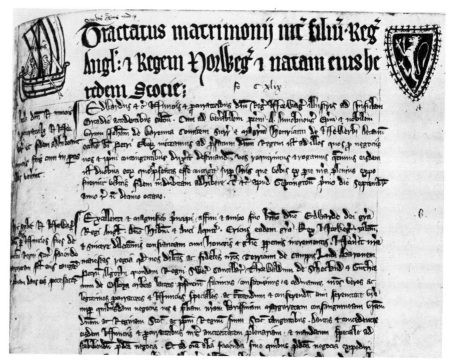

Proposed treaty of marriage, dated 1290, between Edward, son and heir of Edward I of England, and Margaret of Norway, infant granddaughter of Alexander III, who inherited the Scottish throne on his death.

Had Alexander III lived longer, Scotland might have been spared many misfortunes. But in 1286, while he was on his way from Edinburgh to Kinghorn, his horse came down with him in the darkness and he was killed. His first wife, Margaret, both his sons and his daughter, the Queen of Norway, had died before him. A second wife, Yolette de Dreux, whom he had married the year before his death and to whom he was hurrying home when he was killed, had as yet borne him no children. The heir to the throne of Scotland was his grandchild Margaret, the infant daughter of the King of Norway.

Alexander had not long been dead and the little Queen was still in Norway when Edward I Plantagenet of England, a formidable, ruthless man, who had been King since 1272, came forward with the proposal that Margaret should marry his son. In 1290 a treaty of marriage was signed at Birgham and a ship sent to fetch little Margaret, with a consignment of sweetmeats and raisins on board as a present from the English King.

The Treaty of Birgham provided that Scotland should remain a separate and independent kingdom and when Edward proposed that English troops should garrison a number of castles in southern Scotland, the Scots indignantly rejected his suggestion. But it was already clear enough what he had in mind.

The plans of all concerned were, however, now thrown out by the news that the little Queen had died in the Orkneys on her way over from Norway. This laid the succession open to more than a dozen claimants. Of these the two strongest were Robert de Brus or Bruce and John de Bailleul or Balliol. Both were nobles of Anglo-Norman origin with estates in England as well as Scotland. Both were descended on the distaff side from David I's youngest son. And both were personally well known to King Edward I, in whose army they had fought. With so many and such formidable candidates in the field, trouble seemed certain.

Already in October, at the first rumours of the little Queen's death, William Fraser, the Norman-descended Bishop of St Andrews, foreseeing difficulties, had written privately to Edward suggesting that he should come to Scotland to keep the peace and to judge who had the strongest claim to the throne. He also took the opportunity of hinting that John Balliol was likely to prove a docile and amenable neighbour. Edward came and in November 1291, in the Great Hall of Berwick Castle, after much apparent deliberation with eighty Scottish and twenty-four English auditors, announced that the crown had been awarded to Balliol.

The reasons for this choice were clear. Balliol, it is true, had a strong claim to the throne. But Edward also had reason to believe that he would do as he was told. Nor did the English King lose any time in making his demands known. They were that Edward himself should have feudal superiority over Scotland and that Balliol should pay homage to him; that Balliol should, when necessary, come to London to answer any charges brought against him by his own subjects; and finally that Balliol should contribute to English defence costs and join him in his forthcoming invasion of France.

Balliol, not a strong personality, was to go down to history as a nonentity – the Toom Tabard or Empty Coat. But Edward's terms proved too much even for him. Repudiating his allegiance to Edward, he concluded an alliance with France and early in 1296 prepared to invade the north of England.

Edward was waiting for this. His plans were made. Two days after Balliol entered England, he crossed the Border into Scotland. He was met by large numbers of Scottish nobles, many of whom owned estates in England and were

Sterling silver coin of John Balliol, the 'Toom Tabard'.

therefore his vassals. They had come to do homage to him. Amongst them were Balliol's rival, Robert Bruce, and the latter's old father. On hearing this, Balliol seized all Bruce's lands in Scotland and gave them to his own brother-in-law, Red John de Comines or Comyn. The Scots, as so often, were deeply divided among themselves.

Edward next marched on Berwick, at this time the most prosperous city in Scotland, and sacked it, at the same time massacring large numbers of the inhabitants. He then moved on to Dunbar, where, supported by Robert Bruce and other Scottish nobles, he met and utterly defeated Balliol, inflicting terrible slaughter on the Scottish force. Balliol now renounced his crown and after spending three years in the Tower of London withdrew to his estates in France, where he died in 1313.

Edward, meanwhile, continued his relentless progress through Scotland, taking possession of Edinburgh, Stirling, Perth, Elgin and numerous other castles as he went. In August 1296 he returned to Berwick. Here some two thousand Scottish nobles and landholders were compelled to do homage to him and to add their names to the 'Ragman's Roll', a document recognizing him as King. He then left for London, carrying off with him the ancient Crowning Stone of the Scottish kings which Fergus of Dalriada had brought from Ireland seven centuries earlier, and leaving an English Viceroy and English officials to take charge of the administration and English garrisons to occupy the chief strong points. '*Bon bosoigne fait qy de merde se deliver*', was his rude, soldierly comment. The conquest of Scotland was complete. Or so it seemed.

'The Ragman's Roll.' In this copy, on 28th August 1296, one Richard of Horseley signed an oath of allegiance to 'nostre Seigneur le Roi d'Engleterre' in Norman French. In the last few lines, in legal Latin, Andrew, son of the late William of Tang, adds his notarial attestation.

Chapter Two

For some months all was quiet. Then in the spring of 1297, a young Scottish knight from the south-west named William Wallace became involved in a brawl with some English soldiers in the market place at Lanark. With the help of a girl he made good his escape. But the girl – some say she was his wife – was caught and put to death by the Sheriff of Lanark. Wallace resented this. That night he killed the Sheriff and so became an outlaw. Within weeks he was leader of a fast-spreading movement of national resistance. Such movements often spring from small beginnings.

The extent of this movement was forcibly brought home to the English in September 1297, when at Stirling Bridge a large, lavishly equipped and over-confident English army under Edward's Viceroy, Surrey, was completely annihilated by a hard-hitting Scottish force led by Wallace and including

Letter from Sir William Wallace and his lieutenant Sir Andrew de Moray, 'Commanders of the Army of the Kingdom of Scotland', to the Mayors and Communes of Lübeck and Hamburg. It is dated 1297, the year in which de Moray was killed at the Battle of Stirling Bridge.

warriors from all over Scotland. Wallace was now master of southern Scotland. But his triumph was short-lived. At Stirling Bridge he had lost his ablest lieutenant, Sir Andrew de Moray, and now he was to make the mistake, disastrous for a guerrilla, of allowing himself to become involved in a pitched battle against superior forces. In July 1298 he was heavily defeated by Edward himself at Falkirk and never again commanded an army in the field. For another seven years he avoided capture, but in 1305 he was finally caught by the English, taken to London, submitted to a form of trial in Westminster Hall and barbarously executed. For seven years already Edward's armies had ravaged Scotland, using their superior strength to crush any remaining opposition. With Wallace's death it seemed as though resistance in Scotland must finally be at an end.

Robert Bruce

But again appearances were misleading. Amongst the Norman-descended nobles who had paid homage to Edward nine years earlier and served him or seemed to serve him more or less loyally in one capacity or another at different times since, was Robert Bruce, the eighth of his name since the Norman Conquest and the son of John Balliol's chief rival for the throne of Scotland at Berwick in 1291. Despite his long record of service to Edward, Bruce for various reasons of his own, was growing restive. So, too, was John Balliol's nephew, Red John Comyn, now leader of the rival Balliol faction and, like Bruce, a claimant to the throne. So was another Norman noble, Sir Simon Fraser of Tweeddale, who had already been out with Wallace.

Resistance to a foreign occupier is by its nature a complex and secret phenomenon. Evidence is hard to come by and often misleading. Personal motives are varied and involved. The line of demarcation between collaboration and resistance, between treachery and heroism, is not always clearly drawn. Things, in short, are rarely what they seem.

Great Seal of Robert Bruce, on which he is styled 'Rex Scottorum'. He was crowned on Palm Sunday, 1306.

Equestrian statue of Robert Bruce, erected at Bannockburn in 1964, on the 650th anniversary of his greatest victory.

A meeting, presumably to discuss plans for fresh resistance to the English, was arranged between Bruce and Comyn at the beginning of 1306 in the Greyfriars Kirk at Dumfries. Just what passed at the meeting is not known. It seems probable that mutual charges of treachery were made. The ownership of land was also in dispute. All that is certain is that there was a quarrel between the two potential resistance leaders and that Bruce stabbed Comyn and left him dying in the church.

By the standards of the day there was nothing very unusual or indeed particularly disturbing in the murder of one great noble by another. What lent special significance to the incident was that it had occurred in a church and so amounted to sacrilege. This meant that Bruce had at one blow not only involved himself in a blood-feud with the Comyns and their many powerful supporters, but had also incurred immediate excommunication by the Church, an essential ally in any enterprise of the kind he was contemplating. His position was precarious in the extreme.

A lesser man might have decided to lie low and let things blow over. Bruce went to Scone and on Palm Sunday, the 27th of March 1306, raised the Royal Standard and had himself crowned King of Scots. Two days later the crown

Coin of Robert Bruce. Coins from the early part of his reign are rare: not until after Bannockburn was he securely enough established to attend to finance and commerce.

was again ceremonially set on his head by Isobel of Fife, Countess of Buchan. It was her brother's right to crown the King but he dared not do so. She did.

Edward's reply was to send a strong English army to Scotland under Aymer de Valence. On 26 June Bruce was heavily defeated at Methven. His troops were scattered and he himself became overnight a hunted outlaw. The brave Countess of Buchan, who had crowned him, was caught by the English and kept in a cage. Of his other allies, the Earl of Atholl and Simon Fraser were hanged, drawn and quartered, and Fraser's head was put beside Wallace's shrivelled skull on London Bridge.

In these adverse circumstances the great Norman noble showed astounding resilience. He spent the ensuing months in hiding in Arran and Rathlin Island and the Hebrides, in Kintail and Kintyre, in Orkney and possibly in Norway. In the spring of 1307 he returned to find devastation and widespread demoralization. Two of his brothers, who landed in Galloway, were caught and killed. But Bruce and his followers persisted and on Palm Sunday 1307 a first victory followed a year of unmitigated defeat. His principal lieutenant, Sir James Douglas, famous as the Black Douglas and henceforth to be the terror of the English, recaptured his own castle of Douglas from the enemy and utterly destroyed it. Gradually Bruce gathered round him more and more valuable allies: from the east the Celtic Earls of Lennox and Atholl; from the west Angus Og, the ancestor of Clan Donald, and the progenitors of the Campbells and Macleans. Soon other Scottish victories followed: a successful guerrilla action at Glentrool and an encounter at Loudon Hill, where Bruce showed conclusively that his spearmen had the measure of the English heavy cavalry. The English redoubled their efforts and in June Edward I, now a sick man, himself set out for Scotland at the head of a great army with which to subdue his former ally and liege. On 7 July 1307 Edward died at Burgh-on-Sands. With his dying breath he ordered that his bones were to be borne at the head of his army in a leather bag until Scotland had been crushed. But his son Edward II was not the man to carry out his father's injunctions.

For Bruce and for Scotland Edward I's death proved a turning point. Edward II, weak and harassed by domestic preoccupations, soon abandoned his father's project of a major campaign and withdrew, leaving the English garrisons in Scotland to manage as best they could. Bruce now pushed northwards. By the beginning of 1309, after a winter campaign against the Comyns in the north-east and a summer campaign against their allies, the Macdougall Lords of Lorne, during which he seized the Macdougall stronghold of Dunstaffnage, he controlled most of Scotland north of the Forth and Clyde. Later that year, after triumphantly holding a Parliament in Fife, he was secretly recognized as King by the King of France. In 1310 the Church in Scotland came out on his side despite his renewed excommunication by the Pope. By 1311 he was able to invade and devastate northern England, sacking Durham and Hartlepool. During the next three years he drove the English from Perth, Dundee, Dumfries, Roxburgh and Edinburgh, leaving Stirling alone in foreign hands.

It was only now that Edward II really bestirred himself. With a large, lavishly equipped army, he marched north to the relief of Stirling. And there he found Bruce waiting for him.

Bannockburn

The two armies met on midsummer day, the 24th of June 1314, by the Bannock Burn below Stirling. Bruce was outnumbered three to one, but he had chosen his ground carefully. His army, with only a handful of light cavalry

Caerlaverock Castle, Dumfriesshire, besieged and taken by Edward I in his pursuit of Robert Bruce. Later, Bruce recaptured the castle and dismantled it. It was rebuilt in 1583.

and no archers to match the English, was drawn up on higher ground than his opponents. The heavily armoured English knights thus found themselves forced to advance through the waterlogged meadows which bordered the Bannock Burn – 'the evil, deep, wet marsh', as one writer has called it – while the English archers, for their part, had no room to deploy. The battle was joined at sunrise. Long before noon the English were in full flight and their King was making for Dunbar and the border as fast as his horse could carry him.

Henceforward the English made little attempt to keep a hold on Scotland. In 1318 Berwick, their last strongpoint, had fallen and the Scots were free of them. Though the war was to drag on for another fourteen years, its battles were fought outwith Scotland. Bruce now turned the tables on the English, invading and devastating their country as they had devastated his. He also carried the war over to Ireland, whose people, encouraged by what had happened in Scotland, had in 1316 bestowed the Crown of Ireland on his brother Edward. And when in 1322 Edward II in exasperation attempted another invasion of Scotland, he was chased back into Yorkshire, losing his personal baggage in the process.

Nor was Edward much more successful in the spiritual field. Pope Clement V, who had excommunicated Bruce in 1310, was dead, and Edward now invited his successor Pope John XXII to confirm the excommunication. His action provoked a strong reaction from the nobles, clergy and commons of Scotland. Meeting at Arbroath in April 1320, they addressed to the Pope a

Opposite: Representation of the Battle of Bannockburn, from a 15th-century manuscript. It is possible that the man lying on the ground is the Englishman de Bohun, killed in single combat by Bruce himself.

Right: 'The Arbroath Declaration', bearing the seals of all the barons subscribing to its defiant terms. It was executed in duplicate; one copy was conveyed to Pope John XXII at Avignon, while one was retained in Scotland.

notable declaration, in which they proclaimed their devotion to Bruce and to liberty. 'We fight', they wrote, 'not for glory, nor riches, nor honour, but only for that liberty which no true man relinquishes but with his life.' And of Bruce: 'By the Providence of God, by the right of succession, by those laws and customs which we are resolved to defend even with our lives, and by our own just consent, he is our King.' 'Yet Robert himself,' they continued, 'should he turn aside from the task he has begun and yield Scotland of us to the English king or his people, we should cast out as the enemy of us all, and we should choose another king to defend our freedom; for so long as an hundred remain alive we are minded never a whit to bow beneath the yoke of English dominion.'

After receiving this most unequivocal message, the Pope seems to have shown himself rather more forthcoming towards Scotland, and, though still hesitating to recognize Bruce as King, eventually agreed to annul his excommunication. Edward II had failed again. In 1327 he was finally deposed by his wife Isabel and her lover Mortimer and his place as King taken by his young son Edward III.

Further English attempts at invasion came to nothing, only provoking vigorous counter-attacks. The English were by now growing tired of the war. A number of earlier efforts at mediation had failed, but a fresh English envoy was now sent to Norham to sue for peace and in May 1328 a Treaty of Peace between the two countries was signed at Northampton, recognizing Scotland as an independent kingdom and Robert Bruce as her King. At the same time Bruce's baby son David was married to Edward III's little sister Joan.

Just over a year later, in June 1329, at the age of fifty-three, Bruce died at Cardross, some say of leprosy. Human experience shapes human character.

Cast of the skull of Robert Bruce. No contemporary or near-contemporary likeness is known to exist.

The impact of events on the individual cannot be left out of account. Bruce had been transformed by the hazards and hardships, the setbacks and triumphs of the past twenty years which he shared with the ordinary people of Scotland. From an Anglo-Norman noble, an apparently loyal servant of the English King, he had, in twenty years or so, become a Scottish national hero, a leader who by his courage and his will to win had united the people of Scotland as never before and given them a new sense of nationhood.

Now he was dead, leaving an only son, David, aged five years old. His daughter Margery had married a noble of Breton descent, Walter fitzAlan, the Hereditary High Steward of Scotland, also known as Walter the Steward or Walter Stewart or, to give the name its later form, Stuart. At a Parliament held at Cambuskenneth in 1326 and attended for the first time on record by all three Estates, the barons, clergy and representatives of the burghs, it had been decreed that the succession should go first to David and then, in the event of his death without heirs, to Margery's son Robert Stewart. But the future was far from assured.

Most of the men who had shared Robert Bruce's triumphs and achievements were by now either dead or did not long survive him. His brother Edward Bruce and Walter the Steward were both dead. James Douglas was killed fighting in Spain in 1330, while carrying his master's heart on Crusade in fulfilment of a vow. In 1331 little David was crowned King as David II and Bruce's nephew, Thomas Randolph, Earl of Moray, a man of strong character and a good leader, became Regent.

This sword was given by Bruce to Sir James Douglas in token of his last injunction, to go on Crusade to the Holy Land 'and thair bury my hart'. Douglas died on the way.

But already trouble was brewing. In August 1332, urged on by Edward III of England, a number of Scottish nobles, who had been deprived of their lands for siding with the English against Bruce, landed in Fife. Their purpose was to put the Toom Tabard's son, Edward Balliol, on the throne. Moray moved to meet them, but died before the battle was joined. He was succeeded

45

Siege of Perth by the Earl of Mar, a nephew of Robert Bruce who was briefly Regent for the infant King David II. Woodcut from Holinshed's *Chronicles* (1577).

as Regent by the Earl of Mar, another of Bruce's nephews. But Mar was at once defeated and killed in a night attack on Dupplin Moor. The invaders now marched on Scone, where they crowned Balliol king.

It was a situation which invited English intervention. Balliol, intent on appeasement, at once offered Edward III the shire of Berwick as a free gift. But, before he could do anything else, some of his angry subjects under James's brother Archibald Douglas and Andrew Moray of Bothwell had driven him across the border in his shirt and one boot. In the summer of 1333, however, Edward III marched on Berwick in strength, dispersed a French fleet sent to relieve it, heavily defeated the Scots at Halidon Hill and took Berwick. Seeing which way things were going, large numbers of Scottish nobles and clergy now promptly changed sides and joined the enemy, with the result that the Lowlands of Scotland were easily overrun and garrisoned by the English, who filled them with their own merchants, settlers and clergy.

In this confused and dangerous situation David II, now aged ten, and his little English wife, Joan, were sent to France for safety and the Regency en-

David II, not a worthy son of Bruce, is shown in this illuminated miniature shaking the hand of his captor, Edward III, after the Battle of Neville's Cross in 1346. For the next twelve years he enjoyed an easy life at the English Court.

trusted to Bruce's seventeen-year-old grandson, Robert Stewart. The latter, much to his credit, now rallied such resistance as he could and drove the English garrison out of Bute. In 1339, with the help of a French expeditionary force, he captured Perth. By 1340 he had cleared Scotland north of the Forth. And in 1341 he was able to bring his young uncle David back from France and hand over to him the government of the country.

The English were by now fully engaged in France with the Hundred Years War. This gave the Scots a badly needed respite. In addition to Perth, Stirling and Edinburgh were recaptured and Randolph's daughter Black Agnes won lasting fame by her resolute defence of her castle of Dunbar. But in 1346 the French were defeated at Crécy and the King of France appealed to his ally for a diversion. Accordingly in October David II, who was far from being a worthy son of his father, set out with an army for England. There he was soundly beaten at Neville's Cross and himself taken prisoner by the English. David spent the next twelve years in England at the Court of Edward III. He had never been happier, finding that he greatly preferred the easy life of the English Court to the cares and burdens of kingship in Scotland.

In David's absence Robert Stewart once more became Regent. In 1355 the French, again hard-pressed, again asked the Scots for a diversion. This time it

The Scots and their French allies attack Wark Castle, Northumberland. Illumination from Froissart's Chronicles, 15th century.

47

was more successful. Berwick was recaptured and the English badly beaten by William Douglas at Nesbit Muir. Returning from France, Edward III retaliated by invading Lothian, but, though he caused some devastation in the Lowlands, in the end he was forced to withdraw from Scotland with his troops hungry and demoralized.

Edward now tried a new approach. Instead of again attempting to invade Scotland, he made a ten years' truce and, in return for a crippling ransom of 100,000 marks, handed King David back to his subjects. Scotland was in a bad way. David was a useless king. The payment of his ransom debased the coinage and strangled trade. The resulting economic crisis coincided with a period of plague and floods. Across the Channel the war was going badly for France. Demoralization set in. Soon there were those who counselled capitulation to the English. King David, who cared nothing for Scotland, set himself at their head and, returning to England, where he had many friends, made a private arrangement with Edward under which the latter's younger son was to become his heir.

But this arrangement was angrily rejected by the Scottish Parliament and when David's deplorable reign ended with his death in 1371, the kingdom passed, not to the English prince, but to Robert Stewart, the King's nephew and *Robert II* former Regent, who assumed the throne as Robert II, the first Stewart king.

Silver groat (fourpenny piece) of Robert II, first of the Stewart Kings.

Robert had shown himself an adequate Regent, but he proved a weak king. He came, it is true, of a noble family, but one that was no nobler than half a dozen others, was of Norman origin and did not possess the authority or prestige that flowed from eight centuries of kingship. Henceforward a new peril threatened Scotland, that of strife between the nobles and the Crown. It was to be our country's bane through the centuries to come.

This twelve-foot pennant in sage-green silk is the standard of the Douglases, traditionally held to have been carried at the Battle of Otterburn in 1388. It bears a lion passant and St Andrew's cross; the motto 'Jamais areyre' (*Jamais arrière*) refers to the Douglas claim to lead the vanguard of the Scottish Army into battle.

Robert sought to give Scotland peace and prosperity. The English, fortunately for him, had their hands full in France. But the national economy was still strangled by continuing payments on the dead King's ransom and the peace was continually disturbed by the brawling of the great nobles amongst themselves. 'In those days', wrote a contemporary, 'there was no law in Scotland; but the great man oppressed the poor man and the whole country was one den of thieves. Slaughters, robberies, fire-raising and other crimes went unpunished, and justice was sent into banishment, beyond the Kingdom's bounds.' Yet another feature of the reign was continual border-raiding which devastated the whole Border region and culminated in 1388 in the major battle of Otterburn, or Chevy Chase as it came to be called, between the Douglases and the Percys of Northumberland.

In 1390 Robert II died. His son, Robert III, who succeeded him, had been kicked by a horse five years earlier and never fully recovered his health. A well-meaning cripple, he leaned as heavily as his father had done latterly on his younger and more resolute brother, the Duke of Albany. Once again the peace was disturbed by the bickering of the great nobles amongst themselves.

In 1399, Robert III virtually abdicated on the grounds that 'sickness of his person' unfitted him for 'restraining trespassers and rebellers', and for the next twenty-five years Scotland was ruled by Regents. The first of these was Robert's elder son, David Duke of Rothesay. But in the spring of 1402 he was carried off to Falkland and disappeared. Some said that he had died of dysentery; others that his uncle Albany had contrived his disappearance. In any case he did not re-appear and Albany again assumed control, this time as Regent, with his son Murdoch to help him.

The heir to the throne was now Robert III's younger son, James. As rumours were current that the Regent was plotting to hand him over to the English, Robert decided in 1406 to send James to France for safety. But, by ill fortune, the ship in which he was travelling was seized by English pirates from Norfolk. These took him to London and delivered him to the King, Henry IV, who held him as a hostage. The shock killed poor crippled Robert, who died a month later. Little James was now duly proclaimed King James I, but he was destined to spend the first eighteen years of his reign in the hands of the English. Meanwhile his uncle Albany ruled in his stead, and made, as James was the first to notice, very little effort to secure his release. The great nobles, needless to say, made the most of the opportunities presented by this prolonged interregnum, expanding and consolidating their estates, assembling private armies, and building up what amounted to independent principalities of their own.

The Douglases

Of the great lowland families, none surpassed the Douglases, whose power soon came to rival that of the Crown. James, the founder of the family fortunes, had won great glory as one of Bruce's captains. His successor had been made Warden of the Marches and Lord of Galloway by David II. In 1358 an Earldom had been bestowed on the Douglas of the day, and thereafter, by clever marriages, the Douglases had further increased the extent both of their con-

Hermitage Castle, Roxburghshire, most formidable of the Border strongholds, belonged to the powerful Douglases from 1341 to the late 14th century.

nections and of their possessions. By the end of the fourteenth century, the fourth Earl, who was Robert III's son-in-law, possessed lands stretching over Galloway, Douglasdale, Annandale, Clydesdale, Lothian, Stirling and Morayshire. The thousands of fighting men he could muster, toughened by constant border-fighting against the Percys, constituted a power factor that no one, least of all the Crown, could safely ignore.

In the north-west, the Macdonald Lords or, as they styled themselves, Kings of the Isles, continued to enjoy the status of autonomous monarchs, paying little or no heed to the central government of Scotland. Together with their neighbours and kinsmen the Macleans, those 'Spartans of the North', as Andrew Lang has called them, and the Lords of Lorne and Argyll, the Macdonalds had fought with Bruce against the English at Bannockburn. But they had done so as allies rather than as subjects and the Lord of the Isles was now formally allied with the King of England by a series of treaties dated 1392, 1394 and 1398 and signed as between sovereign states. In 1408 this alliance was again renewed when Henry IV of England sent a special embassy to Oxford-educated Donald of the Isles for this purpose.

In addition to the Isles, the Macdonalds, whose power had been greatly strengthened by Bruce's defeat of the Macdougalls a hundred years earlier, already held sway over much of the western seaboard. An opportunity now presented itself for Donald to extend his dominions still further. In 1411 his wife's niece, the young Countess of Ross, entered a convent and renounced her

Tombstone of Ranald, son of the Lord of the Isles, who died in 1386 and was buried on Iona.

Macdonald targes – embossed leather shields on wooden frames, decorated with brass bosses and nails. The one on the left dates to the end of the 17th century; the other (early 18th century) bears the heraldic achievements of Macdonald of Keppoch, who fell at Culloden.

Duart Castle, Mull, a typical stronghold of the clan chiefs – in this case the Macleans.

Carved stone slab from Iona, showing Maclean of Coll carrying a claymore.

Earldom and estates. With these in his possession, Donald could become master of most of northern Scotland. A counter-claim was, however, advanced on behalf of the Regent Albany's son, Buchan, who, as it happened, was also an uncle by marriage of the Countess. Enraged by this and encouraged by promises of help from his ally Henry IV of England, Donald, supported by the Macleans under their Chief, Red Hector of the Battles, marched in strength across Scotland with the object of seizing and sacking Aberdeen. After a preliminary skirmish with the Mackays and the Frasers (now removed from the Borders to north-east Scotland), the Islesmen encountered at Harlaw a mixed force sent to meet them by the Regent and led by Alexander Stewart, Earl of Mar, Sir James Scrymgeour, the Royal Standard Bearer and Constable of Dundee, Sir Alexander Ogilvy, Sheriff of Angus, and Sir Robert Davidson, the Provost of Aberdeen, supported by the armed burgesses of the city. The ensuing battle – the Red Harlaw, as it came to be called – was savage in the extreme and, though militarily indecisive, was nevertheless followed by the withdrawal westward of Donald and his allies, leaving Red Hector dead on the field of battle.

Had things gone otherwise, had the Islesmen achieved their aims, the future course of Scottish history would have been altogether different. As it was, Donald remained quiet until his death in 1423, while the English, who had done nothing to help their ally, now made a truce with Albany. The year 1411, meanwhile, had been marked by a different but important event, the founding of Scotland's first university at St Andrews, to be followed in due course by Glasgow and Aberdeen. Side by side with Scotland's fame as a nation of fighters, a Scottish tradition for learning and the arts was also beginning to

View of St Andrews, seat of Scotland's first university, founded in 1411. *Below*: mace of the Faculty of Arts, St Andrews University. Completed in 1418, it bears the arms of Scotland, and of Bishop Wardlaw, founder of the University, among others.

grow up, a tradition that, fostered in the first place by the Church, brought in its train increasingly fruitful links with Europe and with European places of learning.

Two years later, in 1413, Henry IV of England died and was succeeded by his son Henry V, who, at once seizing the opportunity offered by the civil war then raging in France and by the King of France's madness, attacked France with spectacular success. In 1420 the Treaty of Troyes gave him more than half of France, with the reversion of the rest on the King's death.

But Charles, the French Dauphin, had not surrendered. He now called on Scotland for help. By the beginning of 1421 twelve thousand Scottish troops had arrived in France under Albany's son, Buchan. By the end of March they had turned the tide. At Baugé Henry's brother Clarence was defeated and killed. In 1422 Henry himself died. 'That', he said of the Scots as he lay dying, 'is a cursed nation. Wherever I go, I find them in my beard.' Buchan now became Constable of France and Commander-in-Chief of the French armies, and Douglas was rewarded with the Duchy of Touraine. *Sacs à vin* and *mangeurs de mouton* the French peasants called the Scottish soldiers, impressed by their capacity for food and drink no less than by their fighting qualities.

James I with his Parliament, soon after his return to Scotland in 1424. Woodcut from Holinshed's *Chronicles* (1577).

In 1420 the Duke of Albany had finally died and his place as Regent had been taken by his son Duke Murdoch, a feeble creature by comparison with his father and his brother Buchan. James I, now twenty-nine, was still in England, having spent the whole of his boyhood and youth there. But the way was at last open for his return to Scotland. Old Albany was dead. Henry V was dead. James was on good terms with the Regents who ruled England on behalf of little Henry VI. He was also in love with Henry's cousin, Lady Joan Beaufort, the daughter of the Earl of Somerset. The English, after their experiences in France, were anxious for peace with Scotland. They hoped that James might help them to this end. An agreement was negotiated and in 1424, having married Joan Beaufort, James returned to his kingdom, taking his bride with him.

James I and his Reforms

Having thus at last entered into his inheritance, James lost no time in asserting himself. He possessed great gifts and had been given a good education in England. He had also learnt something of military matters on his visits to the English army in France and of statecraft from personal observation of the methods of those astute and enterprising monarchs Henry IV and Henry V. Furthermore, he had a revengeful and vindictive side to his nature. On his return to Scotland, he found the authority of the Crown weakened, the power of the great nobles dangerously inflated, the administration chaotic, and poverty, lawlessness and pestilence abounding. He took immediate and drastic action. In 1425, as a first step, the Regent Albany, his father-in-law and his two sons were arrested and executed and all their considerable properties seized by the Crown.

The Highlands as usual were stirring. In 1427 James summoned the High-land Chiefs to a Parliament and arrested forty of them. While most were later released, some were put to death. The Highlanders were disgusted by this double-dealing on the part of the King. A year later, to show his resentment, Alexander of the Isles marched on Inverness with 10,000 men and burned it to the ground. James managed to defeat him in battle. But in 1431 the Western clans were out again under Alexander's cousin Donald Balloch of Islay, who again soundly defeated the Earls of Caithness and Mar at Inverlochy, where Caithness was killed. James now once again took command himself, and, thanks to superior numbers and armament, succeeded for the time being in restoring the situation and pacifying the Highlands.

There was trouble, too, in the Lowlands. Again James took vigorous steps to quell it, imprisoning Douglas and driving the rebellious Earl of March into exile. In a dozen years forfeiture and reversion were to give the Crown the Earldoms of March, Fife, Mar, Buchan, Ross and Lennox. Strathearn and Atholl were held by the King's uncle. Douglas and Angus were his neighbours, Moray and Crawford his kinsmen. The balance between the Crown and the nobles seemed well on the way to being restored.

As though to underline this point, the King dressed splendidly, spent lavishly and made Linlithgow Palace into a magnificent royal residence. In 1428, after an unsuccessful attempt to come to terms with England, he formally renewed the Auld Alliance with France and sent a fresh Scottish contingent to fight for Charles VII and Joan of Arc against the English. It was a popular move. 'Nothing', wrote Aeneas Sylvius, the future Pope Pius II, who visited

Aeneas Sylvius visited the elegant and luxurious Court of James I about 1428 on a diplomatic mission. A fresco by Pinturicchio shows him conversing with the King.

55

Scotland at this time, 'pleases the Scots more than abuse of the English.' Aeneas, for his own part, was pleased by the Scottish women, whom he found 'fair in complexion, comely and pleasing, though not distinguished for their chastity'.

James meanwhile had busily embarked on a far-reaching programme of social and legislative reform. 'If God give me but the life of a dog', he had said on first returning to Scotland, 'I will make the key keep the castle and the bracken-bush the cow.' Within a week of his coronation, Parliament was at work on a mass of new statutes, and attendance by the greater and lesser barons was energetically enforced. *Rex Legifer*, they called him, the Law-giver. He even considered the idea of a second chamber on English lines. Not only did he pro-vide for the maintenance of law and order; he regulated the finances of the country; raised new taxes; and introduced a whole range of no doubt badly needed but not necessarily popular reforms. Poaching was prohibited. Salmon fishing out of season was forbidden. Rooks and wolves were to be kept down; football discouraged;* pease and beans planted; hostelries built in the burghs; archery encouraged and improved. James also intervened vigorously in matters ecclesiastical, thus quickly bringing himself into conflict with the Holy See and, incidentally, carrying his point.

It was in the nature of things that such an active king should make enemies. James made three dangerous ones: his uncle, Atholl, his Chamberlain and cousin, Robert Stewart, and Robert Graham, the Tutor of Strathearn, who bore the King a grudge for his treatment of his nephew. Together, these three plotted to kill him, and in Perth, on 20 February 1437, they carried out their plot, stabbing him to death in the presence of his Queen. Joan Beaufort took a terrible revenge on her husband's murderers, but the exceptionally savage and ingenious tortures she inflicted on them, unheard of even in Scotland, could not bring the dead king back to life.

James's son, who now came to the throne as James II, was only six years old. Once again there was a Regency. And once again the great nobles took charge. Parliament was powerless without a strong king and the practice of delegating business to small committees – the Committee of Articles in particular – made it easy for a group of determined men to gain control. The Regent and, as it happened, the next heir to the throne, was the immensely powerful Earl of

---

* Act of 1424: 'Item it is statut and the King forbiddis that na man play at the fut ball under the payne of iiij d.'

Douglas. But Douglas died in 1439, leaving two young sons, and the Regency passed to Sir William Crichton, who had been Master of the Household to James I and Keeper of Edinburgh Castle.

Crichton feared the immense power of the Douglases and in November 1440 he saw a chance to break it. Summoning the young Earl, a headstrong boy of fourteen, and his younger brother to dinner with the little King in the Great Hall of Edinburgh Castle, he caused to be placed before them the symbolic Black Bull's Head, betokening death. He then murdered them both. 'Edinburgh Castle, towne and toure,' sang the poet,

> *God grant thae sink for sinne!*
> *And that even for the black dinoir*
> *Earl Douglas got therein.*

The vast Douglas estates were now divided up and for a time the power of the Douglases was eclipsed.

Armorial bearings and inscription from the tomb of 'James the Gross', seventh Earl of Douglas. He was great-uncle and heir of the young sixth Earl whose murder by Sir William Crichton in 1440 temporarily broke the power of the Douglases.

James II as a young man. Illumination by Jörg von Ehingen.

In 1449, James II, now nineteen, took control of affairs. He was to rule Scotland for just eleven years. During these, loyally supported by Crichton and by his own cousin, Bishop Kennedy of St Andrews, a man of exceptional integrity and strength of character, James was to show himself in many ways his father's son. But he had other things to attend to besides administrative reforms. An alliance, highly dangerous to the Crown, had come into being between the young Earl of Douglas,* who was negotiating with the English, the Earl of Crawford, known as 'Earl Beardie' or the 'Tiger Earl' and at this time the most powerful man in the east, and, last but not least, John of the Isles, still smarting under the affronts which his father Alexander had suffered at the hands of the Scottish Crown in the last reign.

* On his murder in 1440, William, the fourteen-year-old sixth Earl, had been succeeded by his great-uncle, James the Gross, the seventh Earl, who was believed by some to have connived at his great-nephew's murder and who in 1443 was in turn succeeded by his son William as eighth Earl.

Ecclesiastical seal of Bishop Kennedy of St Andrews, James II's cousin and counsellor. It shows the Virgin and Child above, St Andrew in the centre, and the Bishop below with the Kennedy arms. This seal, which was affixed to the Foundation Charter of St Salvator's College, dates to about 1450.

James made some effort to conciliate Douglas. But Douglas rejected his advances. Indeed, he went out of his way to provoke him, while his allies, the Islesmen, again seized Inverness. Finally, in 1452 the King, recalling perhaps a similar scene from his early childhood, invited Douglas to dine with him at Stirling Castle. Douglas came under a safe conduct and over dinner the King stabbed him to death with his own hand. 'The Earl', was the tactful judgment of Parliament, 'was guilty of his own death by resisting the King's gentle persuasion.'

Prospect of the town of Inverness, from Slezer's *Theatrum Scotiae* (1693).

For a time it seemed as though the dead man's four brothers might, with English help, successfully defy the King. But James by his conduct of affairs had won the confidence of his subjects and when in 1455 he forced an issue and marched in strength to meet the rebels, he was abundantly justified by the outcome. James Douglas, the murdered man's heir, fled first to the Isles and thence to England, and at the Battle of Arkinholm his three brothers were defeated and killed. The power of the Black Douglases was thus finally broken and Parliament decreed the forfeiture of their vast estates. Crawford, the 'Tiger Earl', and John of the Isles had already come to terms with the Crown. The kingdom, for the time being, was at peace.

The English, having been decisively defeated in France, were now in the throes of civil strife and their loyalties divided between the rival Houses of York and Lancaster. James, who had made a temporary truce with Henry VI, chose this moment to intervene on his side against the usurper York. The stronghold of Roxburgh, which had been in English hands since 1346, was held by a partisan of York's. In the summer of 1460, James laid siege to it and, as he was watching his guns bombarding it, one of them burst and killed him. A few days later Roxburgh was taken by the Scots and that historic stronghold utterly destroyed.

James III: detail from a triptych by Hugo van der Goes at Holyroodhouse. He was a cultured man with a taste for archaeology and the occult, and for like-minded favourites, but as a king he was ineffective and suspicious. In 1469 he married Margaret, daughter of King Christian I of Denmark and Norway, who brought as her dowry the Orkneys and Shetlands – joined to the Scottish Crown just five hundred years ago.

Scotland was now once again ruled over by Regents. For a short time the Queen Mother assumed the Regency on behalf of her nine-year-old son, James III, but in 1462 her place was taken by Bishop Kennedy, who the following year negotiated a truce with the English, still preoccupied with the Wars of the Roses. Kennedy, however, died in 1465 and was succeeded as Regent by Lord Boyd, an ambitious lesser noble. In 1469 Boyd arranged for the young King's marriage to the daughter of the King of Norway, who brought as her dowry the Orkneys and Shetlands, which thus became part of Scotland. After the wedding, James, now eighteen, himself assumed control of affairs. His first move was to rid himself of Boyd, whose growing influence he resented.

James III did not, however, justify his early promise as a man of action. Though in many ways gifted, he was unsociable and morose, a poor horseman, more interested in architecture, astrology and necromancy than in affairs of state and preferring the company of a group of intelligent and gifted favourites to that of his nobles. This did not endear him to the latter and his reign was punctuated by the usual plots and counterplots, while the English, despite a peace treaty signed in 1474, as usual tried to fish in troubled waters. In all this an active part was at first played by the King's more prepossessing brothers, Albany and Mar, and later by Archibald Douglas, Earl of Angus, head of the Red Douglases, 'who rose upon the ruins of the Black' and had by now replaced the Black as chief menace to the Crown.

In 1479 James, anxious for his crown, imprisoned both his brothers. Mar died mysteriously in prison in his bath. But Albany, having killed his guards, made a spectacular escape from Edinburgh Castle on a rope and, finding his way to London, there assumed the style of King of Scots. Three years later he joined an English army which was preparing to invade Scotland. James set out for the borders to meet the invaders but at Lauder was overtaken by a number of his own nobles. These were led by Archibald Douglas who, while the others hesitated, earned by his forthright approach to the monarch the name 'Bell-the-Cat'. Having hung a number of the King's favourites from the bridge at Lauder,

Margaret of Denmark: detail of the van der Goes triptych.

Two groats of James III. One is unusual in showing the King in half-profile – a Renaissance device. The fleur-de-lys on the reverse of the other symbolizes the long-standing French alliance.

Battle of Sauchieburn in 1488. This mid-19th-century engraving shows Stirling Castle in the background.

Douglas and his friends now returned to Edinburgh, taking the King with them. There they were joined by Albany who, reconciled with his brother, briefly assumed the Regency. The English, for their part, contented themselves with capturing Berwick and then went home, no doubt thinking it wiser to leave the Scots to themselves. Albany eventually fled the country and was killed at a tournament in France. But the King's authority had been badly shaken.

In 1488 a fresh group of conspirators, again led by Archibald Douglas and by Lord Home, and supported this time by Colin Campbell, first Earl of Argyll and Chief of Clan Campbell, managed to lay hold of James's young son, whom they proclaimed King in place of his unpopular father. James hesitated, sought to come to terms with the rebels, called upon them to disband their troops and in the end fled to Stirling, where he found the city gates closed in his face. There was nothing for it now but to stand and fight. On 11 June 1488 the opposing armies met at Sauchieburn, south of Stirling. In the course of the rather half-hearted fighting that ensued James's horse bolted and threw him. Badly injured by his fall, he called for a priest, and a passer-by, who claimed to be one, stabbed him to death as he lay helpless in the kitchen of a mill.*

* There is an old tradition, accepted as authentic by Sir Iain Moncreiffe of that Ilk, that this quick-thinking regicide was none other than William Striveling or Stirling of Keir, a local notable, later to be knighted by his victim's son.

Chapter Three

'THEY SPEND ALL THEIR TIME IN WARS
AND WHEN THERE IS NO WAR,
THEY FIGHT ONE ANOTHER'

James's heir, who now succeeded to the throne as James IV, was fifteen years old. For a time Archibald Douglas exercised a kind of regency and a circular was sent to the Courts of Europe giving a tactful account of the Battle of Sauchieburn, 'whereat the father of our Sovereign Lord happinit to be slane'. Meanwhile Douglas and his fellow-conspirators reaped to the full the rewards of their victory. It is from this time that dates the rapid rise to power of the Argyll Campbells, while Hepburn of Hailes, a minor laird, was rewarded for his services by the titles of Earl of Bothwell and Lord High Admiral.

The young King himself was not without misgivings, remorse even, at the way in which he had been brought to the throne, for the rest of his life he wore an iron chain round his body as a penance. Nor was he one to let himself be ruled by his nobles. When civil war broke out again in the following year, James took the field at the head of his own troops, soundly defeated the rebels, and promptly restored order.

James IV was to prove the ablest and most popular of all the Stewart kings, a *James IV* ruler of energy, intelligence and charm and a born leader of men, whose love for the good things of life was as intense as his religious fervour and the vigour with which he pursued his kingly duties. 'He had', wrote the great scholar Erasmus, who was tutor to one of his many bastards, 'a wonderful force of intellect, an incredible knowledge of all things.' And Pedro de Ayala, the Ambassador of Ferdinand and Isabella of Spain and a constant companion of the King's at the card-table, was impressed by his self-confidence, his physical courage, his religious devoutness and his gift for languages, including the Gaelic. 'The King even speaks', he wrote, 'the language of the savages who live in some parts of Scotland and in the islands.' The people of Scotland, for their part, liked James's

Portrait, believed to be of James IV, of the 16th-century Flemish school.

ostentation, his open-handedness, his friendliness, his many mistresses and his great horde of illegitimate children. For this was before the days of the Calvinist conscience.

It has been rightly said that James stood between two ages. In his reign the Renaissance reached Scotland and its years were marked by a true flowering of learning and of the arts. It was also a period of peace and prosperity and of progress and expansion in a whole range of different fields. In literature this was the age of Robert Henryson and his *Testament of Cresseid*; of William Dunbar's *The Thistle and the Rose*; of Gavin Douglas's translation of the *Aeneid* and Blind Harry's popular epic *Sir William Wallace*. Music, too, became important. James himself played the lute and never travelled without his court musicians and a wide range of musical instruments. Splendid churches were built. In the towns stone began to take the place of wood in the merchants' houses and in the country the great castles ceased to be mere strongholds and took on some of the magnificence of palaces, Falkland, Linlithgow and Craigmillar amongst them. And Ayala was able to tell his King and Queen of the fine furniture and charming gardens and of the elegance of the great Scottish ladies, whose headdress, he said, was 'the handsomest in the world'. Education, though still

'Queen Mary's Harp', a finely decorated Celtic instrument of about 1500.

Linlithgow, one of the more magnificent of the Scottish royal palaces.

Device of Andrew Myllar, who received, in partnership with Walter Chepman, a royal patent to set up Scotland's first printing press in 1507. The device, a pun on Myllar's name, also works his initials into the form of a Greek alpha and omega.

the privilege of the few, increased its impact. More books were imported and in Edinburgh in 1507 a first printing press made its appearance. King's College, Aberdeen, came to join St Andrews and Glasgow as Scotland's third university. A thriving trade, based mainly on Middelburg, grew up with the Low Countries. Scottish raw materials, hides, wool and salted fish were exported against imports of manufactured goods and luxuries from abroad.

Meanwhile in the north-west, beyond the Highland Line, life went on much as it had for five hundred years or more. Here what happened in Edinburgh or in the Anglicized Lowlands had very little relevance. In the Highlands the hold of both Church and State was tenuous in the extreme. Here a different system, different loyalties and different standards prevailed. In Gaelic *clann* meant children. The chief was the father of his people. He was, in theory at any rate, of the same blood as they were. He had power of life and death over them (of which he made full use). And he commanded, by one means or another, their absolute loyalty. His land, in a sense, was their land; their cattle were his cattle. His quarrels (and they were bloody and frequent) were their quarrels. In its

The Clan System

66

essence, the clan system was patriarchal rather than feudal, an ancient Celtic concept which bore but little relation to the more recent central monarchy, but had its origin rather in the early Norse and Irish kingdoms of the west, from whose kings and high kings the chiefs of most of the great clans traced their descent.

To the Highlander, land, the wild barren land of the Highlands, cattle, the stunted little black beasts that somehow got a living from it and from which he in turn got a living, and men, men at arms to guard the land and the cattle, were what mattered. The clan lands belonged by ancestral right to the chief and were sub-divided by him among the members of his family and the men of his clan. The cattle were the most prized possession of chief and clansmen alike, the source of their livelihood and social standing and the source, too, of unending strife. In time of war the chief and those of his own blood led the clan in battle and, when he sent out the fiery cross, it was the duty of the men of the clan to follow where he led. In war and peace alike he had absolute power over them, being, by ancient custom rather than by any feudal charter or legal right, both law-giver and judge. The clan had its foundation in the deeply-rooted Celtic

In the remote north-west, new fashions, new trends in art took a long time to penetrate. The tomb of Alasdair Crotach, seventh Chief of Clan Macleod, was built in 1528, yet the recumbent effigy could almost be that of a medieval knight.

principle of kindness, a mixture of kinship and long tradition, far stronger than any written law. As father of his people, the chief stood midway between them and God, settling their disputes, helping them when they were in need, protecting them and their cattle against their enemies. *Buachaille nan Eileanan* was the Gaelic title of the Macdonald chiefs, the Shepherd of the Isles.

With his chief the humblest clansman shared a pride of race scarcely conceivable to a stranger. All who bore their chief's name liked to believe themselves – and often were – descended, as he was, from the name-father of the clan, from Somerled, from Gillean of the Battleaxe, from Calum Mor, from Olaf the Black or Gregor of the Golden Bridles, and, through them, from countless generations of Norse or Irish kings. 'Though poor, I am noble,' ran an old and constantly repeated Maclean saying; 'thank God I am a Maclean.' And Cameron of Lochiel could boast with conviction that his clan were 'all gentlemen'. 'Almost everyone', the English Lieutenant Edward Burt was to write in amazement some centuries later, 'is a genealogist.'

Little wonder, then, that from their mountain or island fastnesses the great chiefs and chieftains of the north and north-west, surrounded by their loyal clansmen, should through the ages have paid but little heed to the pronouncements of kings or parliaments or officers of state from south of the Highland Line, regarding these only as potential allies or enemies in their own, more personal struggles for power. Which is why, in following the twists and turns of Highland history, it is important to think, not in terms of a clan's loyalty or disloyalty to this or that monarch or dynasty or government, but rather of a system of ever-shifting alliances and conflicts of interest between a number of independent or semi-independent minor kingdoms and principalities. For this is what in fact the clans were.

James, like his predecessors, made an attempt to tackle the recurrent problem of the Highlands and Islands. In 1462, during the previous reign, John, Lord of the Isles, had in his turn concluded an alliance with Edward IV of England, the Treaty of Westminster-Ardtornish. The Estates had subsequently sought to forfeit him, but James III had formally restored the Lordship to him and had hopefully created him a Lord of Parliament. John himself, who was peacefully inclined, might have given no further trouble. But his bastard, Angus Og, who had married Argyll's daughter, took a different view and declared war both on the King and on his father, thus splitting the western Highlands in two and, incidentally, starting a prolonged feud between the Macdonalds on the one hand and the Macleods and Mackenzies on the other. At the Battle of the

The Highland clans in the 16th century: 'semi-independent minor Kingdoms'.

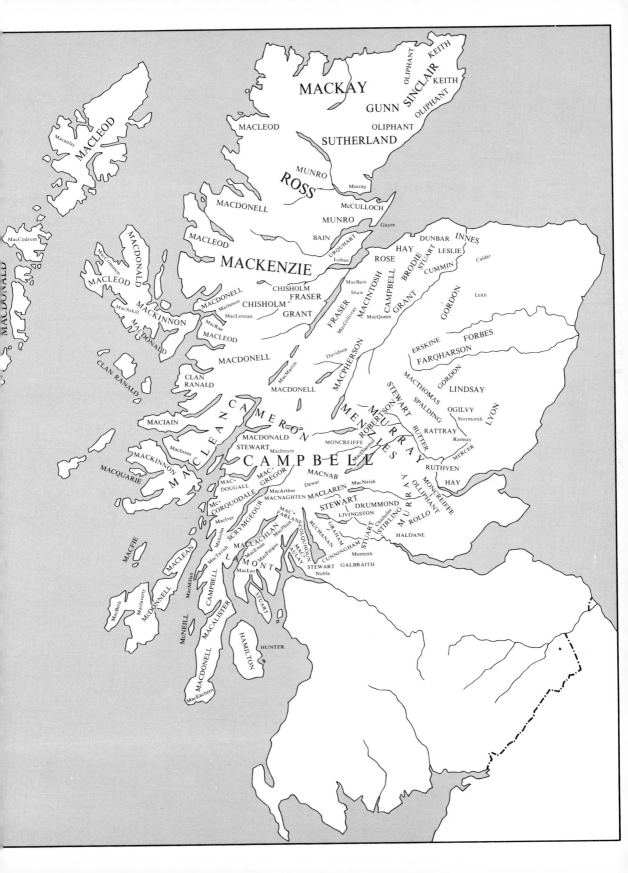

Bloody Bay off Mull, Angus Og in 1480 decisively defeated his father and the latter's chief lieutenants, Maclean of Duart and Maclean of Ardgour, taking all three prisoner. Angus Og was, even for the age, an unusually violent and bloodthirsty man and was only prevented from dispatching his cousin Ardgour on the spot by the timely intervention of Macdonald of Moidart, who was reluctant to see a congenial neighbour obliterated. 'If Maclean were gone', said Moidart, 'who should I have to bicker with?' And for once Angus Og relented. After this Angus Og kept the western Highlands in a turmoil until in 1490 his throat was finally cut by his own harper.

In the following year, the feud between the Isles and the Scottish Crown flared up again. Old John's nephew, Alexander of Lochalsh, setting out from Lochaber, seized the royal castle of Inverness and ravaged the lands of the Mackenzies. The latter, however, defeated him heavily in a great battle at Park and in 1493 the Estates, on discovering that John of the Isles had again been intriguing with the English, finally forfeited the Lordship and annexed it to the Crown. In 1494 old John surrendered and entered a monastery at Paisley. He died four years later, a broken man, in a common lodging-house in Dundee.

James IV now did something that none of his predecessors had done. He made a series of visits to the Isles and the western Highlands, armed and escorted, it is true, but coming as a friend rather than as an invader, making himself known to the chiefs, whose language, as we have seen, he had actually learnt, and feasting and hunting with them. In the hope of keeping them occupied and improving their economic position, he even sought to encourage fishing and shipbuilding. But nothing much seems to have come of this somewhat optimistic project. 'The Scots', reported that shrewd observer Ayala, 'are not industrious and the people are poor. They spend all their time in wars, and when there is no war they fight one another.'

In the end, James, finding the response to his overtures disappointing, reversed his policy, exchanging his patriarchal approach for a more feudal one. Charters were revoked and Huntly and Argyll were made Lieutenants of the Isles and given powers where necessary to feu land to new holders.

This attempt to impose feudal overlords was a mistake. The tutelage of the King's Lieutenants was resented. In 1501 there was another uprising, under John of the Isles' young grandson, Donald Dubh, Black Donald, the son of Angus Og. This culminated in 1503, when the victorious Macdonalds, with the help of the Macleans, again seized and burned Inverness. It was not until 1506 that young Donald was finally hunted down and made a prisoner. In the

Three merchants, unarmed and soberly gowned, reflect the prevalence of peace and order under James IV. 16th-century stone carving.

hope of keeping order, the King now established a number of strategically placed strongpoints throughout the Highlands, at Tarbert and Urquhart, at Inverlochy and Loch Kilkerran. At the same time he greatly strengthened his fleet and substantially increased the number of Sheriffs and Sheriff's Courts.

Meanwhile southern Scotland was for the time being at peace and relatively united. The burghs were more prosperous than ever before. Learning, culture and the arts were making some progress. The outlook for the future seemed hopeful. But appearances were misleading.

Having achieved a measure of peace in his own country the King turned his attention to foreign parts. In the shifting pattern of European alliances, Scotland, her prestige higher than ever, now held, in a sense, the balance of power. James's purpose was to maintain this balance and so prevent a recurrence of the disastrous wars which had ravaged Europe during the past century. Amongst other ideas he nurtured a romantic plan to unite Christendom in a latter-day crusade

71

The *Great Michael*: a model of James IV's warship, built in 1511 at Newhaven, Midlothian.

against the Turks, who, having captured Constantinople, were now sweeping on through the Balkans in an advance which was only to be checked before the walls of Vienna. With this end in view and in furtherance of his active foreign policy, he built a great fleet, for which vast quantities of timber were felled in Fife and at Luss on the shores of Loch Lomond. The *Great Michael* was, or so James believed, the mightiest warship in Europe and Sir Michael Wood and Sir Andrew Barton and his brothers were among the most famous sea-captains of their day.

Basically everything, as usual, depended on Scotland's relationship with her southern neighbour. History showed that a hostile Scotland could hamstring England. For a time James's relations with England had been strained owing to his support of the Yorkist pretender, Perkin Warbeck. But in 1501, at the age of twenty-eight, he had finally agreed to marry Margaret Tudor, the twelve-year-old daughter of Henry VII, a Welsh upstart who in 1485 had usurped the English throne. In February of the following year he signed with England a treaty of perpetual peace – 'a good, real, sincere, true, entire and firm peace, bond, league and confederation on land and sea, to endure for ever.' It was even sponsored by the Pope, who undertook to excommunicate whichever sovereign first broke his pledged word, and in August 1503 James married little Margaret at Holyrood amid scenes of unparalleled splendour, which dazzled, as they were intended to, the grudgingly admiring visitors from south of the Border.

Margaret Tudor, sister of Henry VIII of England and wife of James IV. She had the faults of the Tudors without their brains, and when Scottish and English interests conflicted, as after Flodden, her loyalty to Scotland was doubtful.

But Scotland's new alliance with England did not mean the end of her Auld Alliance with France. On the contrary, in the years that followed James sought consistently to use these two connections to restrain his allies from attacking each other, thus earning the name of *Rex Pacificator*, the Peace-Bringer. Then, in 1511, the Pope, the King of Spain and the Doge of Venice formed what they called the Holy League against France. Their declared aim was her partition. They were joined first by the Emperor and then by James's brilliant but bellicose young brother-in-law, who had recently succeeded to the throne as Henry VIII of England.

France now stood alone save for Scotland. In July 1512 James, convinced that France's survival was essential to the stability of Europe, formally renewed the Auld Alliance. To the last he sought to mediate between the hostile powers.

But it was too late. By April 1513 a European war was in progress and a couple of months later France, attacked on both sides, was in deadly peril. In response to French appeals for help, James sent an ultimatum to Henry VIII. But Henry replied insolently, asserting that he was 'the verie owner of Scotland' which James 'held of him by homage'. Clearly Scotland's own survival was at stake. Mustering the most splendid army a Scottish king had ever commanded, James crossed the Tweed at the head of his troops on 22 August.

Flodden

For a couple of weeks the campaign went well. Four English castles fell to the Scots. Then on a wild afternoon at the beginning of September the two armies met near Flodden Edge under Branxton Hill. For a time it seemed as though the Scots might win the day and at first Lord Home's borderers drove back the English division which faced them. But the English foot soldiers were better armed, their bills outmatching the Scottish spears. The Scots stood their ground and were killed where they stood. In the end the battle became a massacre. The King was slain and with him the flower of Scottish chivalry. Nine earls and fourteen lords, the chiefs of many of the great Highland clans, James's natural son, Alexander, Archbishop of St Andrews, the Bishop of Caithness, the Bishop of the Isles, the Dean of Glasgow and the Provost of Edinburgh and

Signature of James IV on a letter to his 'dearest brother', Henry VIII of England.

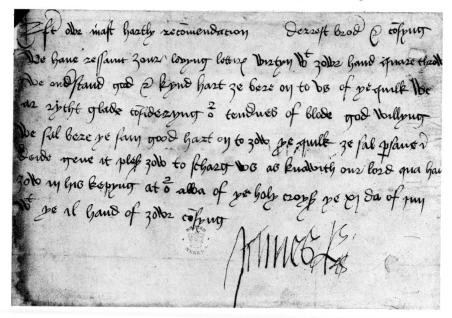

This Standard of the Earl Marischal of Scotland, bearing his motto 'Truth prevails', was carried at Flodden Field. It still shows, 450 years afterwards, traces of blood from the man who carried it.

thousands of Scotland's best young men all perished on that day and their followers with them. Their untimely end is ommemorated in the most moving of all laments: *The Flowers of the Forest are a' wede away.*

After the battle James's body was taken to his brother-in-law, but Henry denied it burial and no one knows what in the end became of it. In his own country there were those who believed that their King was still alive and would one day return to them.

The situation in which Scotland now found herself was extremely precarious. Her King was dead and with him the best of her leaders. Her army had been wiped out. Her only ally, France, was in mortal danger. Across the Border, her old enemy England was triumphant and more aggressive than ever. Her new King, James V, was a baby who could barely walk. Queen Margaret, who now assumed the Regency, had the faults of the Tudors without their brains, and was in any case of doubtful loyalty. Such nobles as had survived Flodden were, with her encouragement, intriguing among themselves. No wonder that an English visitor to Scotland at this time rejoiced at the 'myschefe, robbery, spoiling, and vengeance' which he saw everywhere and prayed God that it might 'continewe'.

But within a year or two things, though still confused, had taken a turn for the better. In 1514 Margaret had forfeited the Regency by marrying the Earl of Angus, head of the powerful Red Douglases, and had been succeeded as Regent by the French-educated and French-speaking Duke of Albany, the son of James III's ambitious and adventurous brother, who had arrived from

France in 1515, determined to continue the traditional policy of a French alliance. France, meanwhile, had been saved from destruction by the divisions of her enemies. The balance had thus been partially restored.

During the years that followed, Albany, supported by the Estates and bolstered by the French alliance, formally renewed in 1517, headed the National or French Party. Against him, at the head of the English Party, stood Angus and Margaret, who were now plotting with Henry VIII to kidnap the little King and carry him off to England. When their plans finally failed, they fled across the Border, though Margaret, after quarrelling with her husband, returned in 1521 to join Albany. Her brother Henry VIII, meanwhile, continued to interfere whenever he could in Scottish affairs and to intrigue against Albany, who in 1524 finally gave up the Regency and returned to France.

Albany's former opponents now started to quarrel among themselves. Angus returned from England and the young King was, in the phrase of a contemporary, 'coupit from hand to hand'. In 1526 James, having reached the age of fourteen, was declared ready to govern. In fact he was to all intents and purposes a prisoner of the Douglases. These, under Angus, had recently routed and slaughtered their rivals the Hamiltons, under Arran, in a pitched battle in the streets of Edinburgh, long to be remembered by its citizens as 'cleanse the Causeway'. They were now masters of the situation.

But two years later, early one summer morning in 1528, James escaped from his captors disguised as a groom, and reached Stirling where some relatively loyal supporters awaited him. 'I vow', said James, after he had escaped from the

Margaret Tudor, James V's mother, and the French-speaking Duke of Albany who succeeded her as Regent. They were two key figures in the intrigue-filled years of James's infancy.

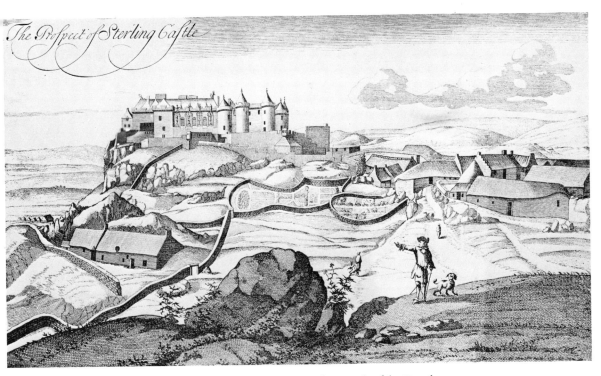

Stirling Castle, to which James V, aged sixteen, escaped from the custody of the Douglases.

Douglases, 'that Scotland will not hold us both.' He was as good as his word. After a sharp clash, Angus was driven across the Border into England, where, needless to say, he was well received by Henry VIII, always glad to welcome disaffected Scots. James, meanwhile, having made a truce with the English, set to work to restore law and order in the Borders and elsewhere. There were, as usual, signs of trouble in the north and north-west, but here also, the young King, thanks to a conciliatory policy, met with a measure of success.

Europe meanwhile was in turmoil. In 1517, four years after Flodden, Martin Luther had nailed his Theses to the church door at Wittenberg. Soon the Continent was to be split into two armed camps. *Cujus regio, ejus religio* was the order of the day. Every sovereign sought to impose his own religion on his own dominions and as often as not on his neighbour's as well. Scotland, once again key to the balance of power, was eagerly sought after. Henry VIII offered James his daughter in marriage. The Emperor Charles V pressed the claims of his sister. Even the Pope proffered his formidable niece, Catherine de Medici. In the end, in 1537, James married Madeleine, the daughter of François I of France. But barely six months later she was dead.

The next year James took another French bride, Marie de Guise-Lorraine. But the two sons she bore him died in 1541. The English, meanwhile, were becoming ever more aggressive. Having himself broken with Rome in 1534, Henry VIII was set on making Scotland Protestant and so turning her against France. But James resisted this. Then in 1542 some Irish chiefs offered James the Crown of Ireland. This gave Henry the pretext he was looking for. Sending his troops across the Border, he followed it up by formally proclaiming himself Lord-Superior of Scotland. James, already ill and at odds with his nobles, replied by invading England. But his nobles refused to march. On 24 November 1542 James's little army, mutinous and feebly led by his favourite, Oliver Sinclair, was defeated at Solway Moss. Sick at heart, the King rode to Falkland and there, two weeks later, received the news that his wife had borne him a daughter. To the dying man this was the last straw. Remembering how the Crown had come to his family through Margery Bruce, 'It came with a lass', he said, 'and it will gang with a lass.' Then he 'gave one little laughtir' and fell back dead. The baby girl, who had been christened Mary, was at once proclaimed Queen.

The Palace of Falkland, to which James V, tired and ill, retired after the Battle of Solway Moss. Here he learned of the birth of his daughter and here, despairing for the dynasty, he died.

James V and his French Queen, Marie de Guise-Lorraine. He was twenty-eight, she twenty-four.

Mary Queen of Scots was less than a week old when she succeeded to the throne in 1542. The outlook was disturbing. By one means or another her great-uncle, King Henry VIII of England, now the principal protagonist of Protestantism in Europe and the sworn enemy both of France and the Pope, was determined to make himself master of Scotland. Ten years earlier he had wanted James V to marry his daughter. Now he sought to win the little Queen as a bride for his sickly son, Edward.

A treaty of marriage was duly negotiated with Arran, the Regent and heir to the throne, who was inclined to favour an English rather than a French connection. But Marie de Guise, the clever and determined young Queen Mother, and her unprincipled but extremely able adviser, Cardinal David Beaton, had other plans. Little Mary was carried off by the Cardinal and crowned Queen at Scone, while the Estates, who rightly distrusted Henry, were without difficulty persuaded to repudiate the treaty of marriage.

Henry VIII's answer was to invade Scotland. During the summer of 1544 Edinburgh and the Borders were laid waste and burnt and appalling atrocities

Marie de Guise.

perpetrated by Henry's soldiers. 'Put all to fyre and swoorde,' ran the Privy Council's instruction, 'burne Edinborough towne, so rased and defaced when you have sacked and gotten what ye can of it, as there may remayne forever a perpetuel memory of the vengaunce of God.' This Rough Wooing, as it came to be known, left in southern Scotland a legacy of hatred for the English which was to endure for centuries. Even the Douglases felt less affection for the English when they found their lands devastated and the tombs of their forefathers destroyed.

Meanwhile in the north-west Henry had found an ally in Angus Og's son, Donald Dubh, Black Donald of the Isles, who, escaping from prison in 1545 after some forty years of captivity, raised, with the help of the Macleans, a force of 8,000 men and 180 galleys to fight against the Government of Scotland and thus show for all to see how little the power of the Isles had been affected by the forfeiture of fifty years before. 'Auld enemys to the realme of Scotland', the Islesmen proudly called themselves.

But the power of the Isles had flared up for the last time. Donald Dubh died the same year in Ireland, leaving no successor. The Islesmen quarrelled over the manner in which Maclean of Duart, as Treasurer of the Isles, had distributed the funds raised to equip the expedition, and the Macdonalds fell out amongst themselves. Henceforward the western clans split along new lines of cleavage and at long last began to show themselves more willing to come to terms with the House of Stewart. In January 1547 death came to Henry VIII of England. But the Duke of Somerset, as Regent for the young Edward VI, continued Henry's policy, sending a fresh army to Scotland which was to inflict a disastrous defeat on the Scots under Arran at Pinkie Cleugh later the same year.

Scotland, meanwhile, had turned to France for help. For the Scots the choice lay more clearly than ever between a connection with Catholic France and one with Protestant England. It was a choice fraught with religious, social and economic, as well as national and political implications. In Scotland, each cause had its adherents. The latest turn of events had driven the Scots for the time being into the arms of France. But it was, for a variety of reasons, an alliance that had come to lack stability.

It was now thirty years since Martin Luther had first published his Theses. Since then Zwingli had founded his Reformed Church and Calvin produced his *Institutes of the Christian Religion*, while in 1534 Henry VIII of England, for reasons not entirely theological, had in his turn embraced Protestantism.

The Watson Mazer, a silver-gilt drinking-bowl, is a fine example of mid-16th-century Scottish craftsmanship. The inscription round the foot can be rendered 'Money lost little lost, honour lost much lost, heart lost all lost.'

To Scotland the Reformation was to come later. Nowhere at this time was the Church more corrupt or degraded. 'Pilates rather than Prelates', Pope Eugenius IV had called the Scottish Bishops. And Archibald Hay, a relative of Cardinal Beaton, had found it necessary to warn him that priests were being ordained 'who hardly knew the order of the alphabet', while others 'come to the heavenly table who have not slept off last night's debauch'. The poet William Dunbar, himself a Franciscan friar, also had something to say about the private life of his spiritual superiors:

> *Sic pryde with Prelatis, so few till preiche and pray,*
> *Sic hant of harlottis with thame, baith nicht and day.*

Though most parish priests were miserably poor, there were eye-catching exceptions. Parson Adam Colquhoun of Stobo lived, we are told, with his mistress Mary Boyd and their two sons, James and Adam, in luxurious ostentation in Glasgow in a manse in the Drygate full of gold and silver, damask and silk, carved and gilded furniture and feather beds, with a striking clock and, in the bedroom, a parrot in a cage.* When Adam died in 1542 his nephew Peter claimed this desirable inheritance, but the parson's two sons,

---

* 'A bird, viz. ane parrok.'

having been formally legitimated in 1530, were duly awarded his entire fortune, including, of course, the parrot. The Bishop of Moray, for his part, provided for all nine of his children at the expense of the Church, while the bastard daughters of rich prelates were much in demand for their dowries. Even Scottish nuns, if we are to believe the reports of Cardinal Sermoneta, 'go forth abroad surrounded by their numerous sons, and give their daughters in marriage dowered with the ample revenues of the Church'. Alexander Stewart, a bastard of James IV, was made Archbishop of St Andrews at the age of eleven as well as Abbot of Arbroath and Prior of Coldingham.

Such a system was, needless to say, not without its advantages to those in authority. In Scotland, the Church was immensely rich, controlling considerably more than half the national wealth. The Scottish Crown in particular received lavish ecclesiastical subsidies from the Pope. And had not His Holiness, at the King's request, obligingly provided priories and abbeys for no less than five of James V's bastards while they were still infants? But for the sincerely religious it offered cold comfort. Everywhere fewer people attended Mass and more churches crumbled into disrepair. 'A great many of the parish churches,' reported the Archbishop of St Andrews, 'their choirs as well as their naves, were wholly thrown down . . . others were partly ruinous or threatening collapse . . . without glazed windows and without baptismal font.'

Successive Provincial Councils, warned by what had happened in England, made some efforts to restore the situation. The root of the trouble, they declared, was 'the corruption of morals and profane lewdness of life in churchmen of almost all ranks, together with crass ignorance of literature and of all the liberal arts.' And this they sought to remedy by statutes: statutes encouraging the clergy to learn to read and to preach in person at least four times a year; statutes laying down 'that neither prelates nor their subordinate clergy keep their offspring born of concubinage in their company nor suffer them directly or indirectly to be promoted in their churches, nor under colour of any pretext to marry their daughters to barons or make their sons barons out of the patrimony of Christ.'

But already it was too late. Though Parliament had banned them, English translations of the Bible were now beginning to be smuggled across the border; they had an immediate, a profound effect. At last people were coming to learn more about the true nature of Christianity; the impact was revolutionary. Everywhere signs of active discontent with the Church became more and more discernible. Soon, by one of those mysterious processes that occur at such times, a spontaneous popular movement of dissent had sprung into being. Of the

THE BIBLE
AND
HOLY SCRIPTVRES
CONTEYNED IN
THE OLDE AND NEWE
Teſtament.

TRANSLATED ACCOR-
ding to the Ebrue and Greke, and conferred With
the beſt tranſlations in diuers langages.

WITH MOSTE PROFITABLE ANNOTA-
tions vpon all the hard places, and other things of great
importance as may appeare in the Epiſtle to the Reader.

FEARE TE NOT, STAND STIL, AND BEHOLDE
the ſaluacion of the Lord, which he wil ſhewe to you this day. Exod.14,13.

THE LORD SHAL FIGHT FOR IOU: THEREFORE
holde you your peace. Exod. 14, vers.14.

.AT GENEVA.
PRINTED BY ROVLAND HALL.
M.D.LX.

Title-page of the Geneva Bible of 1560, one of the first versions of the Bible in English.

critics, some, like the good Bishop Dunbar of Aberdeen, desired reform from within. Others aimed at more drastic changes. Neither group in the event received much practical encouragement from the authorities, whether ecclesiastical or secular.

Of the protagonists of Protestantism in Scotland, one of the earliest and most notable was Patrick Hamilton, a rich young scholar of noble birth and unusual charm. From visits to Paris and to Marburg he had come back to St Andrews a convinced adherent of the new doctrines. On orders from Archbishop James Beaton he was arrested and invited to recant. When in 1528 he refused to do so, he was burnt at the stake outside the Chapel of St Salvator – slowly, for the technique had yet to be perfected. 'My Lord, if you burn any more,' a friend said to the Cardinal, 'let them be burned in cellars, for the reek of Master Patrick Hamilton has infected as many as it blew upon.'

He was right. Patrick Hamilton's death and the courage with which he met it left a lasting impression on many people in Scotland. Soon the new ideas were spreading through the country like wildfire. Nor were the motives of all concerned purely spiritual. To the religious zeal of the reformers were added the greed of many nobles for the rich Church lands and the political enthusiasms of the Anglophile faction.

As a member of the Council of Regency and also a close friend and adviser of the Queen Mother, David Beaton, Abbot of Arbroath and Bishop of Mirepoix in Languedoc, was in a position of great strength. A dissolute man of great experience and ability, he had succeeded his uncle James as Archbishop

George Wishart, of whom it was said that he was 'glad to teach and desirous to learn', preached the Protestant faith in defiance of Cardinal Beaton and Marie de Guise.

John Knox. His formidable personality and fierce eloquence laid the foundation of the triumph of Protestantism in Scotland.

of St Andrews and had with French support also become a Cardinal. Having successfully resisted the attempts of the English to gain control of the little Queen and of Scotland, he and the Queen Mother had next turned their combined energies to the task of consolidating the French connection, while at the same time seeking to check the ever-rising tide of Protestantism in Scotland.

After Patrick Hamilton's death, many of the Protestant leaders had taken refuge abroad. George Wishart, one of the most prominent, had returned to Scotland in 1544, when the persecution of the Protestants was at its height, to resume his preaching and face the consequences. He was accompanied wherever he went by a fervent, grim-looking young priest with a black beard, carrying a large two-handed sword – Father John Knox.

The Rough Wooing was in full swing. It was a time of tension and war, of plots and counter-plots, of mayhem and assassination. Henry VIII had generously offered a thousand pounds for the murder of Cardinal Beaton. John Knox, for his part, had more than once publicly expressed approval of murder, always provided it was from the right motives. Early in 1546 Wishart was arrested on charges of collaboration with the English and participation in a

In 1546 George Wishart was burned at the stake in the presence of Cardinal Beaton – a martyr for the Protestant cause. Woodcut from Holinshed's *Chronicles*.

plot to murder the Cardinal. Knox, who had been his constant companion, had been loath to leave him when danger seemed to threaten him. But Wishart had sent him away. 'Return', he said, 'to your bairns. And God bless you. One is sufficient for a sacrifice.' In March, Wishart, having been convicted of heresy, was duly burned in the Cardinal's presence at St Andrews.

Two months later, in May 1546, the plot to murder Cardinal Beaton was put into effect. His castle at St Andrews was seized by a band of Protestant noblemen and the Cardinal stabbed to death and thrown from his own window. 'Fie! Fie!' were the prelate's last words. 'All is gone.' No one was better pleased to see him go than his old enemy, Henry VIII. An important obstacle to his designs was now out of the way.

Letter from Edward VI of England, nine years old, to his uncle and Regent, the Duke of Somerset, welcoming the news of the Battle of Pinkie – 'the good succese, it hathe pleased God to graunt us against the Scottes'.

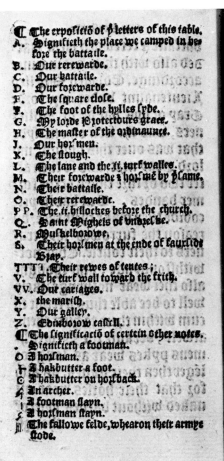

¶ The exposicion of ḡ letters of this table.
A. Signifieth the place we camped in before the battaile.
B. Our rerewarde.
C. Our battaile.
D. Our forewarde.
F. The square close.
F. The foot of the hylles syde.
G. My lorde Protectours grace.
H. The master of the ordinaunce.
I. Our horsmen.
K. The slough.
L. The lane and the ii. turf walles.
M. Their forewarde & horsmen by Plame.
N. Their battaile.
O. Their rerewarde.
P P. The ii. hillockes before the church.
Q. Saint Mighels of Unzelse.
R. Muskelborowe.
S. Their horsmen at the ende of Faurside bray.
T T T. Their rewes of tentes.
V. The turf wall toward the frith.
V V. Our cariages.
X. the marish.
Y. Our galley.
Z. Edinborow castell.
¶ The significacio of certein other notes.
. Signifieth a footman.
O A horsman.
⌐ A hakbutter a foot.
⊙ A hakbutter on horsback.
⌐ An archer.
⌐ A footman slayn.
⌐ A horsman slayn.
⌐ The fallowe felde, whearon their armye stode.

Plan of the Battle of Pinkie, showing the English forces drawn up to the east, the Scots to the west, the Edinburgh side, with the River Esk between.

The Cardinal's assassins now barricaded themselves in the Castle, with John Knox as their rather reluctant chaplain, and, appealing to the English for help, held out there until July 1547, when the Castle was finally reduced with the help of the French fleet, which had arrived off St Andrews at the request of Marie de Guise. Having captured the Castle, the French dispatched to the galleys such prisoners as they took, including young John Knox. The English army, sent by the Regent Somerset, arrived too late to save the garrison, but at Pinkie, six miles outside Edinburgh, managed, as we have seen, to inflict a crushing defeat on the Scots, who, we are told, 'fled . . . like beasts'. In 1549, however, under the Treaty of Boulogne, which ended hostilities between England and France, the English also undertook to withdraw their forces from Scotland.

Until now little Queen Mary had been in Scotland. From Inchmahome Island in the Lake of Menteith she had been moved, for safe keeping, first to Stirling Castle and then to Dumbarton Rock. Now in 1548 she was sent to France, to become, it was decided, the bride of the Dauphin and thus yet further to strengthen the traditional bonds linking Scotland to France. On hearing that agreement had been reached the French King, it is said 'leaped for blitheness'. 'France and Scotland', he declared, 'are now one country.'

In Europe the Protestant movement seemed on the wane. The Council of Trent, by which the Vatican was seeking to regain the initiative, had begun its deliberations. The English had been chased out of France and were withdrawing their troops from Scotland. Their King, Edward VI, though reliably Protestant, was sickly and the succession far from assured. In France Henri II was preparing to crush the Huguenots. The Emperor was getting the best of the Protestant Princes in Germany. In Scotland, finally, Marie de Guise had won over Arran by having him made Duc de Châtelhérault and in 1554 had herself assumed the Regency. Meanwhile Arran's half-brother, John Hamilton, had succeeded Beaton as Archbishop and, however belatedly, embarked on a programme of Church reform.

But in 1549 John Knox had been released from the galleys by his French captors. The hardships he had endured had done nothing to damp his enthusiasm or diminish his energy or conviction. He had first crossed to England, where he had met Archbishop Cranmer, served as Chaplain to Edward VI and been

John Knox preaching to the Lords of the Congregation, the sponsors and signatories of the First Covenant, on the 10th of June 1559. Painting by Sir David Wilkie, 1832.

At the foot of the First Covenant, the first two signatures are those of the Earls of Argyll and Morton.

offered a bishopric. In 1553, on the accession of Mary Tudor to the English throne and England's abrupt reversion to Roman Catholicism, he had gone to Germany and thence to Geneva, where he came strongly under the influence of Calvin. In 1555, fuller than ever of the new ideas and fiercely eloquent, he returned to Scotland. His first target for attack was the Queen Mother, whom he resented not only as a Roman Catholic, but as a woman. The Bishops cited him, but finally decided to drop the charge. His impact was formidable. Even Marie de Guise herself was half fascinated by him. In 1556 Knox went back to Geneva, where Calvin had now set up a model state on Calvinist principles, and there attended to the spiritual needs of the local English community. In 1559 he was to return to his own country for good.

Already, despite Marie de Guise, the Protestant movement in Scotland was now rapidly gaining ground. The numbers of active Protestants were increasing and they were becoming more demanding. In 1557 a powerful group of nobles led by Argyll and Morton drew up the document which was to be known as the First Covenant and for which signatures were sought all over Scotland. In this the Lords of the Congregation, as its sponsors were called, pledged themselves

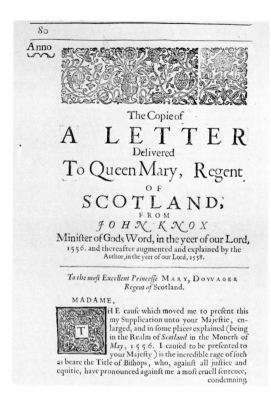

The Copie of

A LETTER

Delivered

To Queen Mary, Regent

OF

SCOTLAND,

FROM

JOHN KNOX

Minister of Gods Word, in the yeer of our Lord,
1556. and thereafter augmented and explained by the
Author, in the yeer of our Lord, 1558.

To the most Excellent Princesse MARY, DOVVAGER
Regent of Scotland.

MADAME,

T HE cause which moved me to present this
my Supplication unto your Majestie, enlarged, and in some places explained (being
in the Realm of *Scotland* in the Moneth of
May, 1556. I caused to be presented to
your Majesty) is the incredible rage of such
as beare the Title of Bishops, who, against all justice and
equitie, have pronounced against me a most cruell sentence,
condemning,

The Catholic Queen Mother, Marie de Guise, was John Knox's prime target of attack when he returned to Scotland in 1555, fired by the influence of Calvin. This open letter to her, of the following year, puts the case against 'such as beare the Title of Bishops'.

to 'establish the most blessed word of God' and to 'forsake and renounce the congregation of Satan', in other words to break with Rome and set up a reformed national Church. In particular, they insisted on the Communion in both kinds, on the public exposition of the Scriptures and the holding of religious services in the vernacular on the lines laid down by the new English Book of Common Prayer. They won widespread popular support. But neither Parliament nor the clergy would meet their requests. And there were signs that the Regent, now sure of help from France, was preparing to take a more intransigent line.

Of late, the burning of Protestants as heretics had become much less frequent. In April 1558, however, the Catholic hierarchy, possibly feeling that things were going too far, decided to make an example of Walter Myln, an aged priest of eighty-two, who was accordingly sent to the stake at St Andrews. But the event aroused so little enthusiasm locally that in the end the Archbishop's servants had to burn him themselves for want of volunteers. He was, as it turned out, the last Protestant to be burned in Scotland as such.

A few days later, at a magnificent ceremony in the Cathedral Church of Notre Dame de Paris, the fifteen-year-old Queen Mary was married to the

Dauphin of France. The two countries were now more closely linked than ever. Henri II graciously granted French citizenship to all Scots who came to France and Frenchmen in Scotland were accorded reciprocal privileges. An eventual union of the crowns and the virtual conversion of Scotland into a province of France seemed probable. Indeed before her marriage the young Queen had already signed documents placing her kingdom in pledge. In Scotland, however, many viewed the course events were taking with apprehension and murmured louder than ever against the Queen Mother.

It now became clear that Marie was proposing, with all the resources of the State behind her, to suppress the Covenant by force. Soon feeling in Scotland ran high. Early in 1559, in response to pressing requests from the powerful Protestant faction, John Knox returned. His sermons were more stirring and inflammatory than ever. He seemed possessed of an almost daemonic power. All over central Scotland, in Perth, at St Andrews, in Stirling and Linlithgow, excited mobs, inflamed by his eloquence, set to work breaking up churches, smashing altars and destroying religious statues and pictures. The scene seemed set for civil war.

In November 1558, meanwhile, had come the news that the Catholic Mary Tudor was dead, leaving the English throne to her Protestant half-sister, Elizabeth. The Scottish Protestants could once more hope for help from England. Moreover Queen Elizabeth's personal interests were very much involved. In July 1559 Henri II died and Mary's husband François succeeded to the throne

The death-bed of Henri II of France. His son, the Dauphin François, and his daughter-in-law Mary Queen of Scots were at the bedside (by the foot of the bed).

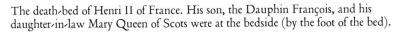

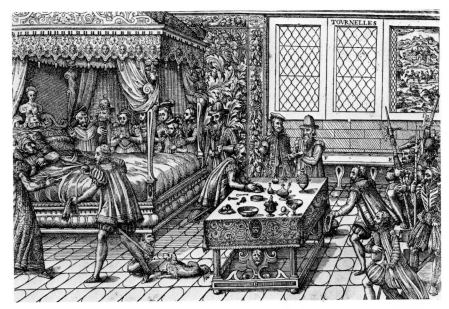

of France. No sooner had he done so than he proceeded to quarter the arms of France with those not only of Scotland but also of England thereby openly announcing his claim to both crowns. For in Roman Catholic eyes Elizabeth was only the natural daughter of Henry VIII and Mary, as the grand-daughter of Henry VII, could rightfully claim the throne of England as well as that of Scotland. It was a warning which Elizabeth Tudor knew how to take and which was greatly to influence her subsequent attitude towards her young cousin.

Encouraged by the renewed triumph of the Reformation in England and by the prospect of English support, the Scottish Protestants redoubled their efforts. All the churches in Perth were sacked and the Mass forbidden on pain of death. The Queen Mother now sent the Earl of Argyll and Lord James Stewart, Mary's own half-brother, to reason with the rebels. But all they did was themselves to join the insurgents and, though Knox himself spoke chidingly of 'the rascal multitude', still more churches were sacked. Marie could only appeal for more help from France.

John Knox and 'Goodman' blowing the 'First Blast of the Trumpet'. In his Protestant zeal, Knox feared 'no Queene in her Kingdome'. Woodcut from a contemporary Dutch account.

It was in these circumstances that Elizabeth of England opened negotiations with the Scottish Protestants. She did so reluctantly, for she disapproved of rebels on principle and, as a woman, particularly disliked John Knox and the title of his latest work, *The First Blast of the Trumpet against the Monstrous Regiment of Women*. 'To promote a woman', ran one passage, 'to bear rule, superiority, dominion or empire above any realm, nation or city is repugnant to Nature; is contumely to God.' Knox, for his part, was no more enthusiastic. But neither party had any doubt in their minds that France's claims to the thrones of England and Scotland must be firmly rebutted. Accordingly the astute Maitland of Lethington was sent to London to negotiate the Treaty of Berwick and early in 1560 an English fleet appeared in Scottish waters and the Queen Mother's French forces, sent by the Guises to support their sister, fell back on Leith. Here, besieged by an Anglo-Scottish army four times their size, they bravely held out for another six months.

The year 1560 marked a turning point in Scottish history. In June, Marie de Guise died. Her death removed from the scene a powerful influence on affairs. Early in July the Treaty of Edinburgh recognized Elizabeth as Queen of England and provided for the withdrawal from Scotland, not only of all English, but of all French troops. In effect it put an end to the Auld Alliance and ensured the ultimate victory of Protestantism in Scotland. It also marked the first step towards ultimate union with England.

In August Parliament was called. By successive statutes, the authority of the Pope in Scotland was abolished and the celebration of the Latin Mass forbidden. And now John Knox, who had seen his ideas triumph, was, with five others, given the task of formulating the creed and the constitution of the new Church. These were embodied in *The Confession of Fayth* and *The First Book of Discipline* to which was later added *The Book of Common Order*, to be known as 'Knox's Liturgy'. These documents were to provide for a time the foundation for Protestant worship in Scotland.

Protestantism Prevails

THE
FIRST BOOKE
OF DISCIPLINE.

To the great Councell of Scotland now admitted to the Regiment, by the providence of God, and by the common consent of the Estates thereof, Your Honours humble servitors and ministers of Christ Iesus within the same, wish grace, mercy, and peace from God the Father of our Lord Iesus Christ, with the perpetuall increase of the holy Spirit.

From your Honours we received a charge dated at Edinburgh the 29. of April, in the yeare of our Lord 1560. requiring and commanding us in the name of the eternall God, as we will answer in his presence, to commit to writing, and in a book deliver to your wisedomes our judgements touching the reformation of Religion which heretofore in this Realme (as in others) hath been utterly corrupted: upon the receit whereof (so many of us as were in this towne) did convene, and in unitie of minde doe offer unto your wisedomes these subsequents for common order and uniformitie to bee observed in this realme concerning doctrine, administration of Sacraments, election of Ministers, provision for their sustentation, Ecclesiasticall discipline, and policie of the Church; Most humbly requiring your Honours, that as you look for participation with Christ Iesus, that neither ye
                                                                        admit

Knox's *First Booke of Discipline*, in 1560, marked the triumph of the Protestant Church in Scotland, and the 'reformation of Religion which heretofore in this Realme (as in others) hath been utterly corrupted'.

Frontispiece to the 'Tennowr' part of the First Psalm, from *The Scottish Psalter*, 1566, by the Reformer, Thomas Wode, Vicar of St Andrews.

Compared with other countries, the Reformation in Scotland had made few martyrs. In all, seven Protestants suffered death by law before the Reformation and two Catholics after it. The majority of the Catholic clergy either joined the new Church or retired on pensions, while their flocks for the most part followed suit. In the old Church corruption and decay had more than done their work. It fell apart almost of its own accord. The time for killing was to come later, when the finer points of Protestant doctrine were ripe for debate. But, whereas in England the Reformation had been a matter of botched-up compromises and equivocal half-measures, in Scotland it was radical. Calvin's relentless logic saw to that. Henceforth the Church of Scotland was governed not by a hierarchy of Bishops and Archbishops, but by Kirk Sessions of lay elders and later by district Presbyteries, possessing the power to ordain the Ministers. The General Assembly of the Kirk, meeting once or twice a year to settle questions affecting the Church as a whole, soon became a forum for Scottish opinion on secular as well as on ecclesiastical matters. Provision was made, too, for a new national system of education. Every parish, in theory at any rate, was to have its school, an ideal that in practice long remained unfulfilled.

Under the influence of Knox and, indirectly, of Calvin, the early Kirk was austere in character. With time this austerity increased still further. Soon

Mary Queen of Scots, in mourning for her father-in-law Henri II of France. Portrait by François Clouet, probably painted in 1559.

Christmas and Easter were no longer observed and Knox's liturgy was abandoned in favour of spontaneous prayer. Singing was unaccompanied. The churches were unadorned. Holy Communion, which Knox had intended should be central to the life of the Church, was celebrated less and less frequently. Throughout Scotland the influence of parish ministers became paramount in lay as well as Church matters and Kirk Sessions exercised widespread influence. Though there were notable exceptions, austerity became the keynote of Scottish life, both social and religious.

It was to this austerely Protestant Scotland, the Scotland of John Knox, that Mary Queen of Scots returned in August 1561. Her husband had died in the previous December. No longer Queen of France, she was still Queen of Scotland. And now, young, beautiful, light-hearted, high-spirited, highly-sexed, impulsive, French in education and outlook, a devout Roman Catholic and a widow at eighteen, she came to claim her inheritance. Clearly the situation was fraught with the most explosive possibilities.

From the first, Mary let it be known that, while she had no intention of abandoning her own faith, she equally did not intend to impose it on her subjects. Indeed she went out of her way to surround herself with Protestant nobles and advisers; she wished to reign as Queen of Scots and not as leader of

95

Henry Stewart, Lord Darnley, at the age of seventeen. Two years later, in 1565, he married Mary Queen of Scots, four years his senior.

a faction. But this was of no great help to her. The Protestant divines were scandalized by Mass being celebrated in Holyroodhouse, not to mention what they regarded as the frivolous conduct of the Queen and her Court. They were equally dismayed when the Protestant nobles who had seized the rich properties of the old Church kept them for themselves instead of letting them be made over to the new.

Then in 1565, Mary fell in love with, or at any rate decided to marry, her worthless cousin, Henry Stewart Lord Darnley, a not very intelligent, teenaged Roman Catholic of notoriously bad character, four years younger than herself. On 29 July 1565 they were married according to the Roman Catholic rite and Darnley was proclaimed King. They had not been married for twelve months when Darnley became jealous of the influence of the Queen's Italian secretary, Riccio, and, with some friends, murdered him in her presence. This greatly

David Riccio, the Queen's Italian secretary and favourite, was murdered in her presence by Darnley and a band of armed men. Oil painting by Sir William Allan, 1833.

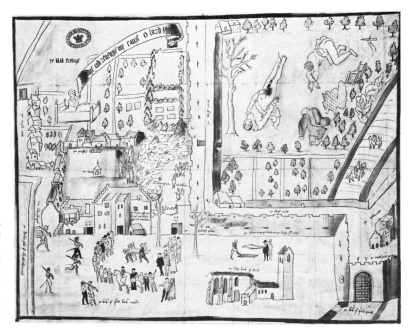

The murder of Darnley at Kirk o' Field in 1567. At top right the bodies of Darnley and his page, stripped of their clothes by the explosion; below, the funeral procession and the burial. Even the roof of the church was shattered by the explosion.

distressed Mary, who was six months pregnant. It also turned her against her husband. In 1567 came the news that Darnley's house at Kirk o' Field, near Edinburgh, where the Queen had sent him to convalesce from a distressing, some said disgraceful, disease, had been blown up and his body found amid the wreckage. On closer inspection, he proved to have been strangled.

No one ever discovered just who had murdered Darnley. But it was obvious to all that James Hepburn, fourth Earl of Bothwell, the Lord High Admiral, a bold, reckless Protestant of considerable charm, but of the most deplorable reputation, was heavily implicated. Eight weeks later Mary married him according to the rites of the Protestant Church.

James Hepburn, Earl of Bothwell.

Mary Queen of Scots.

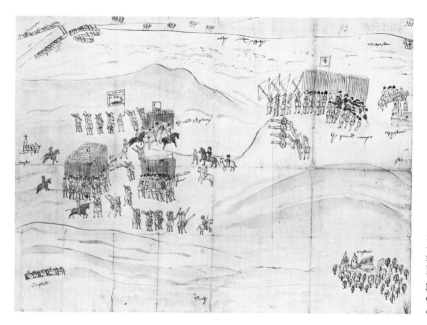

Contemporary drawing of the Battle of Carberry Hill. On the right, Bothwell sits on horseback behind the Catholic guns. In the centre, Mary, also on horseback, is led away defeated.

Whatever its motivation, this further error of judgment alienated both Protestants and Catholics alike and finally cost Mary her throne. Scotland was in turmoil, a prey to intrigue and violence. Within a month the Protestant Lords had raised an army on the pretext of saving the Queen from Bothwell and at Carberry Hill had successfully taken her from her followers. After being led, in a short red petticoat, through the streets of Edinburgh amid derision, Mary, who was still only twenty-four, was in June 1567 forced to abdicate in favour of her baby son, who was immediately crowned King as James VI. The sermon on this occasion was preached by John Knox. Bothwell escaped to Norway and Mary's Protestant half-brother, James Stewart, who was one of James V's more intelligent, if devious, bastards and had been made Earl of Moray, was now appointed Regent. He was, and remained, in close touch with the English Court.

After Carberry Hill Mary was held for some months a prisoner in Loch-leven Castle. Thence in 1568 she escaped by boat, with the connivance of the Hamiltons who had plans of their own for her and, taking her to Hamilton Palace, again helped her to raise an army. But again she was defeated, this time at Langside by her half-brother, Moray. In desperation she now crossed the Solway and in May 1568 threw herself on the mercy of the Queen of England, who, never for a moment forgetting her cousin's claim to the English throne, promptly imprisoned her. 'Strike or be stricken,' was Elizabeth's motto. 'Strike or be stricken.'

Opposite: In Fotheringhay Castle Mary Queen of Scots, a prisoner of Queen Elizabeth, wrote verses on blank pages of her Missal, signing them – in spite of her forced abdication – 'Marie R.'

qu cama lauantage eust contraire le sort
la vie m'est moins vtile que la mort
t plus tost que chager de mes mans l'act
hacune change pour moy d'humeur et de
l'octobre aduertir nature

Marie
R

come autres fois la renomee
ne vole plus par l'uniuers
cy borne son cours diuers
a chose d'elle plus aimee
vous

Marie R.

Les heures ie guide & leuar
par l'ordre de ma mere
fuittant mon triste seiour
pour y croistre ma lumiere

celle qui d'honneur faut combler
hacun de u bruit de sa louange
neu peux moins fu a soy resemble
en effet n'estant que un bel aye
faut plus que la renomee

The KINGS mote

576. Foot high

The GENERALLS

Chapter Four

'THE GREAT MARRIAGE DAY OF THIS NATION WITH GOD'

The years that followed Mary's abdication and flight were troublous ones for Scotland – years of disquieting signs and wonders. 'In this time', we read in the *Diurnal of Occurrents* for 1570, 'there was ane monstrous fish in Loch Fyne, havand greit ein in the heid thairof, and at sumtymis wald stand abune the watir as heich as the mast of ane schippe; and the said had upoun the heid thairof two crowins, the ane abuve litel and the dounmaist crown mekill: quhilk was reportit be wyse men that the same was ane signe and taikning of ane suddain alteration within the realm.'

It was a safe enough conclusion for the wise men to draw. While James VI, who had been barely a year old at the time of his coronation, was growing up under the care of his learned but disagreeable tutor George Buchanan, who methodically thrashed and overworked him, the country was once again ruled by a succession of Regents. Mary's supporters, meanwhile, the 'Queen's Lords', who were working for her return, had seized Edinburgh Castle and were holding it against all comers. The first two Regents, Moray and Lennox, were murdered one after the other. Mar died in office. It was not until 1573 that the next Regent, Morton, a sworn enemy of the Queen, succeeded, with the help of heavy cannon brought from England, in capturing the Castle and ousting its

George Buchanan

Opposite: English troops under Sir William Drury besieging Edinburgh Castle, held by Sir William Kirkcaldy for Queen Mary, in 1573.

Right: James Stewart, Earl of Moray.

Far right: James Douglas, Earl of Morton.

James VI as a boy: portrait by Arnold Bronkhorst. Crowned King at a year old, motherless, brought up by a harsh tutor, he was the victim of a tug-of-war between Catholics and Protestants until he escaped from captivity and proclaimed himself King in fact as well as in name, at the age of seventeen, in 1583.

garrison. Then in 1578 Morton himself was overthrown and two years after that, in 1581, impeached and executed on the charge, strange to say, of having, fourteen years before, murdered Darnley.

Morton's removal was the work of Esmé Stewart, Seigneur d'Aubigny, a fascinating Franco-Scottish cousin of the little King's, for whom the latter had formed a sentimental attachment and whom he now created Duke of Lennox and Lord High Chamberlain of Scotland. This was the first of a series of such attachments which persisted throughout the reign and did nothing to improve the image of the monarchy.

While publicly repudiating his own Roman Catholicism, it now became Lennox's purpose to make a Catholic of James and use him to head a Catholic rising in Scotland and England, with French and Spanish help. In this he was frustrated by a group of strongly Protestant nobles led by the Earl of Gowrie and by Morton's nephew Angus, who in 1582, with the aid of English funds, kidnapped the King, in what was known as the Raid of Ruthven, and took over the government of the country themselves. Lennox now fled back to France and died there a few months later. Much relieved, the General Assembly approved the raid and in Edinburgh a great concourse sang the 124th Psalm: 'Our soul is escaped as a bird out of the snare of the fowlers.'

In 1583, however, James, who was now seventeen, escaped from Ruthven and from his captors and, accompanied by a single servant, made his way to St Andrews where he proclaimed himself King in fact as well as in name. One of his first actions on assuming power was to execute the Earl of Gowrie, who had held him prisoner at Ruthven and had since again sought to get him into his power. Seventeen years later the pattern was, strangely enough, to repeat itself when, in mysterious circumstances, yet another kidnapping, or alleged kid-napping, of the King was followed by the sudden demise of yet another Earl of Gowrie, the son of the first.

James VI of Scotland

Despite a promising start, the young King had difficulty in controlling his nobles and his favourites and the early years of the reign were further marred by civil strife and by the brawling of the Catholic and Protestant factions and various combinations and permutations of the two. But, though the experiences of his childhood and youth, going right back to the pre-natal impact of Riccio's murder, might have been enough to unbalance a stronger character, James, for all his faults and foibles (which were considerable and included a persistent obsession with witchcraft and witches), was to grow up a man of taste, education and intelligence who, as a monarch, lacked neither shrewdness nor political skill.

Like others of his line, James VI aspired not to be the leader of this faction or that, but 'universall King'. Some of his subjects, notably the Ruthvens, thought him too generous in his treatment of the Roman Catholic Earls of Huntly, Erroll and Angus, whose rebellions constantly disturbed the north of Scotland at this time, and whose assassination of the Bonny Earl of Moray, a popular Protestant, was blamed by many on the King, who let Huntly off with no more than a week's imprisonment. But James, quite apart from his personal con-victions, had very good reasons for remaining a Protestant. So long as he did so, and so long as he stayed on reasonably good terms with his cousin Elizabeth of England and with her powerful Secretary, Sir Robert Cecil, he had every reason to hope that on her death he would succeed to the English throne, a rich

During her long imprisonment, Mary Queen of Scots worked this embroidered hanging, in silk on canvas. The hand holding a pruning-hook, and the motto, 'Virtue flourishes with wounding', may indicate a philosophical acceptance of her fate. Her initial and that of her first husband François are intertwined on the left.

prize by any standards. And so in 1585 he concluded an alliance with England and when in 1587, after holding her a prisoner for nineteen years, Elizabeth finally executed his mother Mary for alleged complicity in a plot to assassinate her, he made a formal protest, but did no more, though his subjects, impulsive as ever, and enraged by what they regarded as an insult to Scotland, loudly clamoured for war against the hereditary enemy. With Robert Cecil, in particular, James henceforward kept up a constant secret correspondence and received from him much useful advice and encouragement.

Execution of Mary Queen of Scots at Fotheringhay Castle in 1587. The ostensible reason was complicity in a plot to assassinate Queen Elizabeth.

James VI and his Queen,
Anne of Denmark,
daughter of Frederick II
of Denmark and Norway.

In 1589 James travelled to Oslo to marry Anne of Denmark, a suitably Protestant princess. But there was no money to celebrate their homecoming in what he considered suitable style. 'For God's sake,' he wrote to a well-disposed minister, 'take all the pains ye can to tune our folks well now against our homecoming lest we be all shamed before strangers. Thus recommending me and my new rib to your daily prayers, I commit you to the only All-sufficient.'

The principal problem that now faced James was that of the Kirk. The issue was no longer the old religion or the new, but just what form the new religion should take, and in particular whether the Church should be governed, as in England, by bishops appointed by the Crown or by Assemblies of ministers and laymen. For the Scottish Reformed Church had a very different tradition from the English. It had come into being not thanks to the Crown, but in spite of the Crown. And that tradition persisted.

Though a convinced Protestant, James was no Presbyterian. Indeed, presbytery stood for everything he most disliked. He himself was strongly attached to the idea of episcopacy. 'No Bishop,' he would say, 'no King.' And he was equally strongly opposed to any suggestion of interference by the Church in the affairs of the State.

In 1581 *The Second Book of Discipline* had been declared authoritative by the General Assembly. This represented a success for the ideas of Andrew Melville, the religious leader on whose shoulders the mantle of John Knox had fallen after the latter's death in 1572. But while Melville equalled Knox in zeal and vehemence, his theological views went a good deal further than those of his predecessor. He was in particular more strongly opposed to episcopacy than Knox had ever been and even maintained that Church Courts should instruct civil magistrates in their jurisdiction, quoting divine authority in support of this view. In other words he claimed that the Church should direct the affairs of the State and not vice versa. He did not even accord the King the respect which James felt was his due. 'God's sillie vassal', he called him, to his face.

In 1584 James, who saw in bishops (who were appointed by him) a convenient means of enforcing his own will, retaliated by inducing Parliament to pass statutes confirming the appointment of bishops and forbidding Convocations of ministers save by leave of the King. These measures encountered immediate and vigorous opposition and in the end James was forced to give way. Though bishops of a kind still held office, Presbyteries, Synods and General Assemblies were once again allowed to meet.

There ensued, under the aegis of Andrew Melville, a fresh trend towards extreme Calvinism. Opposition to episcopacy increased still further and, as part of the reaction against a formal liturgy, extempore prayer began more and

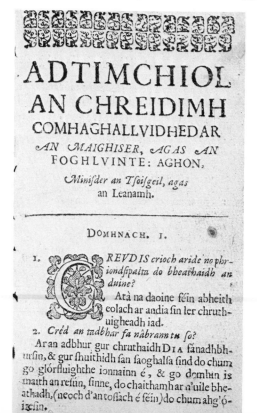

Calvin's *Catechism* was translated into the Gaelic by John Carswell and published in Edinburgh in 1631. Title-page of the first edition.

Bristling with symbolism, this triumphal arch was erected for the entry of James VI into London as James I of England. At the top are the figures of Peace and Plenty; below them, supporting a globe, are Gold and Silver, flanked by Pomona and Ceres. To left and right of these, the Nine Muses and the Seven Liberal Arts make flattering reference to the new monarch's intellectual attainments.

more to replace the forms of worship provided for in the Book of Common Order. But these opinions were by no means universally held. A strong body of Protestant opinion, led by Archbishop John Spottiswoode and strongly supported by the King, took the opposite view. 'I am verily persuaded', wrote Spottiswoode, 'that the government episcopall is the only right and Apostolique form. Paritie among ministers is the breeder of confusion, as experience might have taught us, and for these ruling elders, as they are a mere human devise, so they will prove, if they find way, the ruin both of Church and estate.' The religious conflict inherent in these two opposing Protestant views was to grow in violence throughout the seventeenth century, colouring this whole period of Scottish history, and persisting scarcely diminished until our own times.

Meanwhile for James the fulfilment of all his dearest wishes was at hand. At the end of March 1603 came the long-awaited news that Elizabeth of England had died and that he had been declared her heir. Robert Cecil had not failed his friend. On 5 April James set out for London. Though he continued to speak broad Scots for the rest of his life, he was only once again to return to Scotland.

James I of England

Coronation of James VI and I and his Queen in Westminster Abbey – a splendid ceremony, to judge from this contemporary engraving, but a hurried one as there was plague in London at the time.

James thoroughly enjoyed the new life which now began for him. He liked the pomp and the luxury, the flattery of the obsequious English courtiers and the rich magnificence of the English Court. He liked the way the English did things. And, above all, he liked the Church of England with its abundance of bishops and its elaborate ritual.

As for the affairs of Scotland, he would ideally have favoured a union of the two Kingdoms as well as of the two Crowns and, whenever he could, used the name Great Britain to cover both, while the new joint flag bore the name of Union Jack. In 1607 the Estates, after due debate, passed an Act of Union. But in the end no treaty was signed. James's English subjects had no wish to merge their identity with that of their northern neighbours and viewed with abhorrence the idea of a joint Parliament. 'The Scots', said Sir Charles Piggott, Member of Parliament for Buckinghamshire, censoriously, 'have not suffered above two Kings to die in their beds these two hundred years.' And so the Union was rejected.

Henceforward James's orders went forth in writing from Whitehall to the Scottish Privy Council, and by them and by the Committee of Articles, who to all intents and purposes now controlled Parliament, were promptly carried out. 'This I must say for Scotland,' was his comment, 'here I sit and govern it with my pen. I write and it is done, and by a Clark of the Council I govern Scotland now, which others could not do by the sword.'

Not that James was opposed to the use of armed force against his compatriots when he considered it necessary. It was his ambition in particular to pacify the Highlands, where the old Celtic culture still persisted and the clans pursued their ancient feuds without much regard for what happened further south. This he sought to do largely by issuing Letters of Fire and Sword, which authorized one or more clans to deal with their erring neighbours in the manner they thought best – generally a very rough one. The method, it must be admitted, was not ineffective. Thus, orders came from London for the extirpation by their hereditary enemies of the notorious Clan Gregor, the destruction of their homes, and even the extinction of their name, which the remaining survivors of this operation were no longer allowed to bear. At the King's behest, too, the Macdonalds of Islay suffered frightful punishment, while his own cousin, Patrick Stewart of the Orkneys, or Earl Pate, as he was known, he had publicly

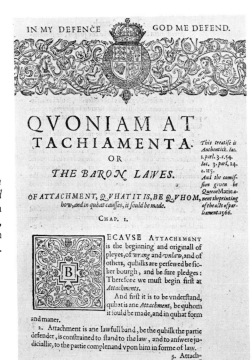

Page from Sir John Skene's *Regiam Majestatem, The Auld Lawes and Constitutions of Scotland*, 1609 – an account of the Scottish legal system, which was as different from the English then as it is today.

109

hanged. Finally in 1608 Maclean of Duart and a number of chiefs of the other Island clans were invited on board one of the King's ships for the purpose of hearing a sermon, and then, by a characteristic stratagem, carried off and imprisoned. The following year, after they had been released on giving pledges of future good behaviour, they were summoned to a kind of peace conference under Andrew Knox, the able new Bishop of the Isles, and invited to sign a document entitled the Statutes of Iona. These were intended to discourage, amongst other things, begging, drinking and the use of firearms and also committed the signatories to reduce the numbers of their own entourage, to dispense as far as possible with the services of clan bards and to send their sons to be educated in the Lowlands. It also placed on a more regular footing relations between the chiefs and the Scottish Crown. The chiefs duly signed the document set before them and for a time things were quieter in the north-west. Henceforward, in particular, no more was heard of the claims of the Lords of the Isles to be independent sovereigns. The days when the Macdonalds could look to Westminster for support were past. James played the Macleans off cleverly against them and they now took their place among the other western clans as equals and not as overlords, and suffered, as did their neighbours, from the rapid rise to power of the Campbells of Argyll, who now emerged more and more as the agents of the central Government and the protectors of the Lowlands against the warlike clans of Lochaber and the west.

James also had a rod in pickle for the Presbyterians. For some years after 1603, the General Assembly was not allowed to meet. Then, in 1606, Andrew Melville, with seven other Ministers, was on some pretext summoned to England, rigorously interrogated, imprisoned for three years in the Tower of London and then forbidden ever again to return to Scotland.

Having thus removed the principal obstacle to his designs, James now increased the powers and numbers of the Scottish bishops. By 1610 there were eleven bishops and two archbishops, one of whom was John Spottiswoode. For the time being the King did not seek to interfere with the prevailing form of congregational worship, which was perhaps why the opposition to his religious policy was not more widespread. In 1617, however, he decided to take matters further still and himself set out for Scotland for the first time for fourteen years. The appearance in the Chapel Royal of Holyrood of carved heads of the Saints, of an organ – a 'Kist o' Whistles', as the disgusted citizens called it – and of *Five Articles* surpliced choristers was not popular. Nor were the Five Articles which the King now sought to impose: that Holy Communion should be received

James VI of Scotland, I of England. Portrait dated 1610, school of Marcus Gheeraerts the Younger.

kneeling; that the festivals of the Christian year should be observed; that confirmation should be administered by bishops and not by ministers; that private baptism and private Communion should be allowed in case of serious illness.

But James was determined to have his way. A General Assembly was summoned to meet in Perth in 1618 and the Five Articles pushed through. They met with widespread and vigorous opposition, and a systematic boycott throughout most of Scotland. Men would walk miles rather than take Communion in a 'kneeling' church. The dispute was to be a long drawn out one.

But James's life was now approaching its end. By 1624 he was mortally ill and the control of affairs had passed to the last of his male favourites, the Duke of Buckingham, and to his son Charles, who had become heir to the throne on the death of his elder brother Henry. In 1625 James died and Charles I began his ill-fated reign.

Charles I
Charles had been born a Scot and was accordingly regarded by his English subjects as a foreigner. But he had left Scotland when he was three and did not return there until 1633, the eighth year of his reign. He thus had but little understanding for Scottish affairs or Scottish opinion. Neither the Highlands nor the Lowlands, with their diverse and highly individual traditions and social systems, meant much to him. A devout Anglican and Episcopalian like his father, he disliked what he knew of the Kirk and of Presbyterians. He also shared his father's distrust of democratic assemblies, whether Scottish or English, and, like him, believed profoundly in the Divine Right of Kings, especially as applied to himself. He did not, however, possess his father's natural caution nor his statecraft. His chief duty towards Scotland, as he in all sincerity saw it, lay in bringing the Scottish Kirk into line with the Church of England. And this he now set out to do.

As a first step he decreed in 1625, by the Act of Revocation, the restoration to the Church of the Church lands and tithes which had been distributed among the nobles – the Lords of Erection, as they were called – at the time of the Reformation, his purpose being to make adequate provision for the maintenance of the Scottish clergy. This no doubt well-meaning measure earned him the distrust of the nobles without winning him the support of anybody else, and, even when a compromise solution was eventually arrived at, the early suspicions still lingered. An outright demand in 1629 that religious practice in Scotland should conform to the English model further alienated all sections of opinion in Scotland and further increased his unpopularity. Nor was this all.

Charles I on the occasion of his first
visit to Edinburgh in 1633. He was
crowned in St Giles's with full
Anglican rites, and soon the word
'Popery' was on men's lips.

In 1633 Charles came to Scotland to be crowned, accompanied by William
Laud, his new Archbishop of Canterbury. The Coronation Service was held
in St Giles's with candles, crucifix, genuflecting bishops and full Anglican
rites. Edinburgh was made a bishopric with St Giles's for Cathedral. Archbishop John Spottiswoode was appointed the King's Chancellor for Scotland.
Ministers were advised to wear surplices. The General Assembly had not met
since 1618 and presbyteries were now threatened with dissolution. Soon feelings
were running high and the word 'Popery' was on men's lips.

It was in this atmosphere that the King and Laud raised the most explosive
of all questions, that of the liturgy. They had by now begun to realize that the
English Prayer Book, unaltered, could never be acceptable to the Scots and a
Commission was accordingly appointed to draw up a Revised Prayer Book for
Scotland, its purpose being to take the place of extempore prayer.

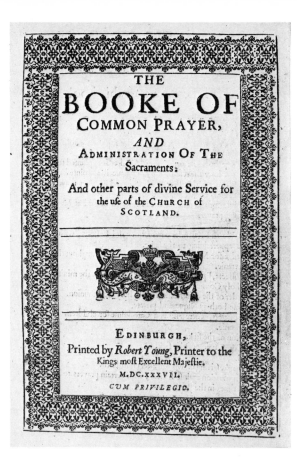

THE
BOOKE OF
COMMON PRAYER,
AND
ADMINISTRATION OF THE
Sacraments;

And other parts of divine Service for
the use of the CHURCH of
SCOTLAND.

EDINBURGH,
Printed by *Robert Young*, Printer to the
Kings most Excellent Majestie.
M.DC.XXXVII.
CVM PRIVILEGIO.

The Revised Prayer Book for Scotland (*left*) was read
for the first time in St Giles's in 1637, and caused riots.
An etching by Wenceslaus Hollar (*below*) shows one
such scene: the air is thick with flying missiles as the
'Arch-Prelate', in full canonicals, reads from the
loathed book. *Opposite:* among leading Protestant
opponents of King Charles's innovations were two
prominent ministers, Alexander Henderson of Leuchars
(*left*) and James Guthrie of Stirling.

The Arch-Prelate of St Andrewes in Scotland
reading the new Service-booke in his pontificalibus
assaulted by men & women, with Cricketts stooles
Stickes and Stones.

The new book was read for the first time in St Giles's on 23 July 1637 amid scenes of violence and disorder which soon developed into a regular riot, in which the female members of the congregation, egged on according to tradition by a certain Jenny Geddes, played a leading part. Before long the resulting disturbances had reached such a pitch that the Privy Council were obliged to shut themselves in Holyroodhouse to escape from the mob, while the Bishop of Brechin, for his part, found it advisable to conduct Divine Service with a pair of loaded pistols laid in front of him in full sight of the congregation. On receiving in London the Privy Council's report of what was happening, the King, who by now had many other no less serious cares and preoccupations and but little time to devote to Scottish affairs, simply sent back instructions that all who had protested against the Prayer Book should be punished and its regular use enforced.

In Edinburgh, meanwhile, opposition to the Prayer Book was becoming daily more formidable and better organized. During the autumn and winter of 1637 a committee was formed in Edinburgh known as the Tables. It included the Earls of Montrose and Rothes, Lord Warriston, an eminent lawyer, some influential ministers, in particular Alexander Henderson of Leuchars, and numerous other notabilities, both clerics and laymen. Known to be in sympathy with them were Lord Lorne, heir to the Earl of Argyll, and Sir Thomas Hope, both Privy Councillors.

But the King, oblivious as usual of the strength and fervour of the opposition he had aroused and as usual out of touch with opinion in Scotland, persisted stubbornly in the course on which he had embarked. To the petitions against the Prayer Book now coming in from all over the country, backed by men of the utmost weight and substance, he responded by sending orders that the petitioners should be dispersed and punished. Finally in February 1638, before leaving for Newmarket to hunt, he issued from London a proclamation, to be read in public in Edinburgh and other cities, summoning the nobles who had resisted the Prayer Book to submit to the King's will and conform.

This brought matters to a head. There were angry demonstrations at the Mercat Cross. The Tables recalled the Lords of Congregation, and on 28 February and the two days that followed several hundred representatives of the nobles, the gentry, the burghs and the clergy flocked to Greyfriars Kirk in Edinburgh to sign a document which had been drawn up by Lord Warriston, Alexander Henderson and others, and which was to be known as the National Covenant. 'The great Marriage Day', Warriston called it, 'of this Nation with God.'

The National Covenant

The Covenant was a skilfully drawn-up document, calculated to attract the maximum of support. It incorporated the Negative Confession of 1581, which specifically condemned a number of characteristic Catholic doctrines, and also appended a whole catalogue of Acts confirming it. It showed how these had been contravened by the latest 'inovations' and protested against their violation. And it ended with a pledge on the part of the signatories to maintain 'the true religion' and, it may be observed, 'His Majesty's authority'. For the leaders of the movement did not want, at this stage at any rate, to come out openly against the King, but only to convey to all and sundry the impression that he was badly advised.

Soon mounted messengers were carrying copies of the Covenant all over the Lowlands and thousands of signatures were being collected. The country-side was in a ferment. National feeling was deeply aroused. In the eyes of many the Covenant possessed more than purely theological significance. It was also a defence 'against our poor country being made an English Province'. And so opposition to the Covenant was vigorously discouraged and ministers who refused to read it from the pulpits were in due course deposed.

During the summer of 1638 contact of a kind continued between London and Edinburgh. But Charles suffered, as he was bound to, from being an absentee sovereign and his Commissioner, the Duke of Hamilton, an unpopular

A creased and crumpled sheet of parchment (below), closely written on both sides, symbolizes Scottish rejection of the Divine Right of Kings in favour of man's duty to God. This is the National Covenant, drawn up in February 1638; copies were carried all over the Lowlands, and thousands of signatures were collected, at their head those of Montrose and the Earl of Rothes (left).

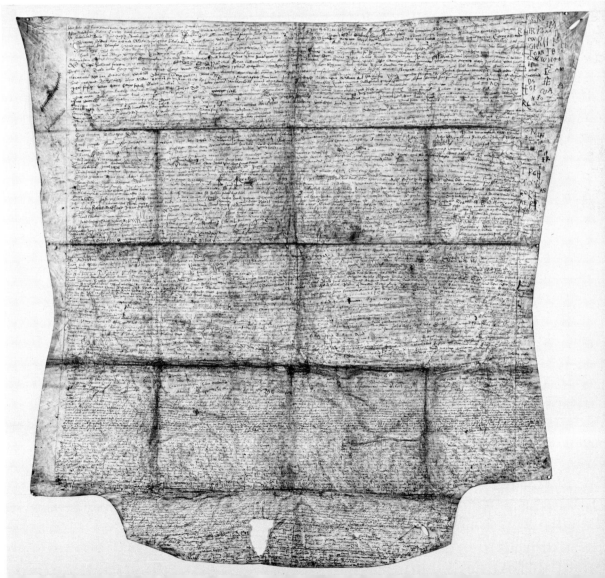

James Graham, fifth Earl
of Montrose, leader with
Sandy Leslie of the
Covenanters' army.

figure at the best of times, carried but little weight. Already the Tables had become the *de facto* government of Scotland.

The King, now thoroughly alarmed, had already told his English Privy Council in July that he would have to use force. In order to gain time, however, he now agreed to a meeting of the General Assembly in Glasgow. This was called for November 1638, and at once got down to business. The Assembly knew its own mind. All bishops were deposed or excommunicated, the Prayer Book, roundly condemned as 'heathenish, Popish, Jewish and Arminian', was abolished and a Commission set up to investigate abuses. To this the King simply replied that none of the Assembly's decisions were valid because they had been reached in the absence of his Commissioner, who had walked out at an early stage in the proceedings. An open breach was now inevitable.

Meanwhile, in Scotland enthusiasm for the Covenant was growing. In the east this was largely inspired by the young James Graham, fifth Earl of Montrose, whose influence extended through Stirlingshire, southern Perthshire, parts of

Archibald Campbell, first Marquess of Argyll and chief of Clan Campbell.

Angus and even into Aberdeen, where Episcopalianism and resistance to the Covenant were most deep-seated. In the west, the Covenant's chief supporter was Archibald Campbell, eighth Earl of Argyll, the powerful Chief of Clan Campbell, a convinced Calvinist, deeply distrustful of the King.

All that summer arms had been coming into Scotland from abroad and Scottish soldiers serving overseas had been returning to their own country 'in gryte numbers upone hope of bloodie war'. In Alexander Leslie, the 'old, little, crooked soldier' who had fought against Wallenstein in Germany and eventually succeeded Gustavus Adolphus in command of the Swedish Army, the Covenanters had an outstanding and experienced general. The King, for his part, was in a less favourable position. He had an inefficient administration, no standing army and no general worthy of the name.

In the early summer of 1639, however, Charles, having somehow assembled a poorly trained force of some twenty thousand men, moved to the Border. At Berwick he came face to face with a far better trained, better disciplined and above all better commanded force under Sandy Leslie. Neither side wanted to fight and the First Bishops' War, as it was called, was eventually brought to an end by the so-called Pacification of Berwick, under which the King agreed that all disputed questions should be referred to another General Assembly or to Parliament.

The new General Assembly's first move was at once to re-enact all the measures passed by the Glasgow Assembly. Parliament, when it met, went further still, defying the King and his Commissioner, abolishing episcopacy and ultimately freeing itself from royal control. In particular, steps were taken to ensure that the Committee of Articles, by which the King had long controlled Parliament, should cease to be a mere tool of the Sovereign.

A Second Bishops' War followed speedily. This time the Scots under Leslie and Montrose crossed the border and quickly captured the important English cities of Newcastle and Durham. Once again the King, whose disorderly rabble had melted away before the Scottish onslaught, was obliged to negotiate. For this purpose and also in order to raise funds, he found it necessary to summon his English Parliament, something which, to all intents and purposes, had not been done for more than ten years. It was to prove a fateful step. For the Parliament which at his behest now assembled in Westminster was to be the famous Long Parliament.

By summoning Parliament Charles gave his English enemies the chance for which they had long been waiting. The King's Government at once came under severe attack and his chief supporters, Strafford and Laud, were impeached and in due course executed. Civil war threatened.

It was now the autumn of 1641. In the hope of winning Scottish support Charles came to Scotland, where he distributed a number of titles, making Leslie Earl of Leven and promoting Argyll to Marquess, and as part of a package deal, accepted all the decisions of the General Assembly of 1638 as well as those of the Scottish Parliament of 1641. Finally he formally gave Parliament the right, of which it had long been making full use, to challenge the actions of his ministers.

Civil War

Events were by now fast reaching a climax and in August 1642 came the news that civil war had actually broken out in England between the King's forces and those of Parliament. The Scots at first held aloof. The principal purpose of the Covenanters was not political but theological. They were concerned to secure the suppression of episcopacy and the establishment of presbytery, not only in Scotland, but in England and Ireland as well. And they

The Government of Charles I: a contemporary engraving shows this to consist of the King in Council, the Lords Spiritual and Temporal, the Commons and – strangely in modern eyes – the Convocation of the Church. To none of them did Charles pay much attention.

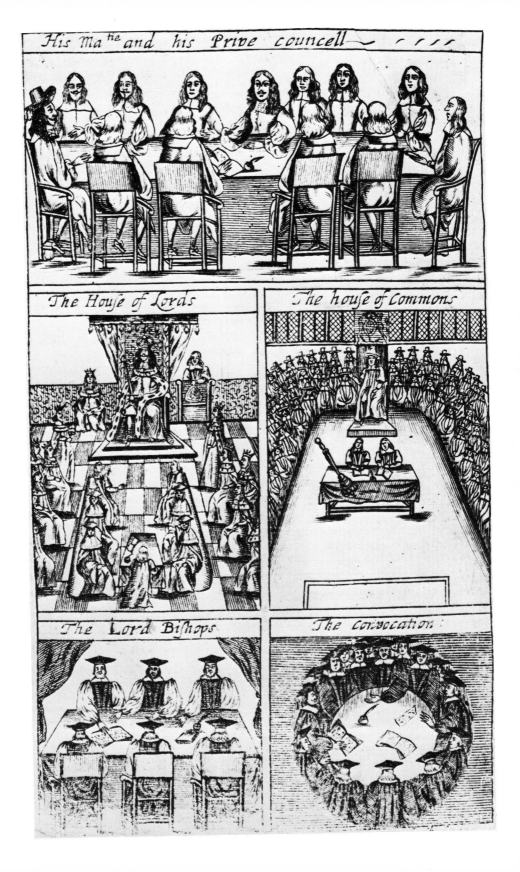

were prepared to give their support to whichever party promised them this. They were also far from agreeing amongst themselves.

In the Kirk, meanwhile, extremist tendencies were gaining the upper hand. To read passages from the Bible at funerals 'bred', it was now held, 'debosherie'. To repeat the Lord's Prayer in public was a sign of Popery. To take cognizance of Christmas or Easter was a special abomination. At the same time it began to appear to Montrose and others that the newly created Marquess of Argyll was exploiting the situation to further his personal interests and consolidate his personal power. Montrose, while remaining a Presbyterian and an upholder of the Covenant, accordingly now took his place at the head of the Moderates and with some of his supporters signed a pact at Cumbernauld, reaffirming both his belief in the Covenant and also his loyalty to the King.

In England, meanwhile, one Royalist victory had followed another until, in the summer of 1643, the Parliamentary leaders, facing defeat, decided in their turn to go to Scotland for help. The English Parliament had one considerable inducement to offer the Scottish Covenanters. While on the whole satisfied with the state of religion in Scotland, the latter had the gravest doubts about the religious practices of their English and Irish neighbours. Moreover, although they had deeply resented the King's attempts to bring Scottish religious practice into line with that of England, they saw nothing wrong in seeking to reverse the process. Negotiations were accordingly opened and in the autumn of 1643 an agreement known as the Solemn League and Covenant was signed by representatives of the Scottish Covenanters and of what was left of the English Parliament. Under the terms of this strange document the Covenanters undertook to attack the Royalist forces from the north – this in return for the sum of £30,000 a month and an undertaking that there would be 'a reformation of religion in the Kingdoms of England and Ireland in doctrine, worship, discipline and government, according to the Word of God and the examples of the best reformed churches, and that popery and prelacy should be extirpated'. In the eyes of the Scottish signatories there was no necessity further to define the phrase 'the best reformed churches'. It could only mean one thing.

The English now set out to fulfil their part of the bargain by summoning the Westminster Assembly. This was a mixed body of clergy and laymen, including eight Scottish delegates, and was entrusted with the exacting task of establishing uniformity of worship in Scotland, England and Ireland. Ironically enough, this predominantly English body, while leaving but little trace of its deliberations in England or Ireland, was to have a lasting influence on Scottish

i 6   a Solemn   4 3

LEAGUE AND COVENANT,

for Reformation, and defence of
Religion, the Honour and happinesse
of the king, and the Peace and safety, of the
three Kingdoms of
ENGLAND, SCOTLAND, and IRELAND.

in a perpetuall Covenant
that shall not be forgotten.

We Noblemen, Barons, knights, Gentlemen, Citizens, Burgesses, Ministers of the Gospel, and Commons
of all sorts in the Kingdoms of England, Scotland, and Ireland, by the Providence of God living vnder
one king, and being of one reformed Religion, having before our eyes the Glory of God, and the advance-
ment of the kingdome of our Lord and Saviour Iesus Christ, the Honour and happinesse of the kings Ma-
iesty and his posterity, and the true publique Liberty, Safety, and Peace of the Kingdoms, wherein every
ones private Condition is included, and calling to minde the treacherous and bloody Plots, Conspira-
cies, Attempts, and Practices of the Enemies of God, against the true Religion, and professors thereof in all places, especially in these three kingdoms ever since the Reformation of Religion, and
how much their rage, power and presumption, are of late, and at this time increased and exercised; whereof the deplorable state of the Church and kingdom of Ireland, the distressed estate of the Church and kingdom of England, and the dangerous estate of the Church and kingdom of Scotland, are present and publique Testimonies; We have now at last, (after other
means of Supplication, Remonstrance, Protestations, and Sufferings) for the preservation of our
selves and our Religion, from utter Ruine and Destruction; according to the commendable practice of those kingdoms in former times, and the Example of Gods people in other Nations;
After mature deliberation, resolved and determined to enter into a mutuall and solemn Legue
and Covenant; Wherein we all subscribe, and each one of us for himself, with our
hands lifted up to the most high God, do sweare;

In the summer of 1643 the Parliamentary leaders turned to Scotland for help. The price of Scottish aid: £30,000 a month and a Solemn League and Covenant to establish uniformity of worship in the three Kingdoms of England, Scotland and Ireland, according to the examples of 'the best reformed churches'.

religious thought and practice. To this day the Westminster Confession of Faith serves as the basis for Presbyterian worship in Scotland. It is also interesting to recall that the original version of the metrical psalms, which have since played so large a part in Scottish life, also came from England, having been produced by the then Provost of Eton, a Cornish Member of Parliament named Francis Rous.

For Charles the conclusion of the Solemn League and Covenant meant serious trouble. Early in 1644 a Scottish force of 26,000 men crossed the Tweed under the command of David Leslie, a distant kinsman of Alexander's. And in the following July, largely thanks to Scottish help, the Parliamentary forces, now re-organized under Oliver Cromwell, were able to inflict a heavy defeat on the Royalists at Marston Moor in Yorkshire.

At this critical juncture, however, the King gained a new ally. For some time past Montrose had been finding himself less and less in sympathy with his

Oliver Cromwell,
Lord Protector.

Prospect of Old Aberdeen. When Montrose captured it for the King in 1644, his hungry Highlanders and his Irish mercenaries looted this prosperous University town and murdered its burgesses.

fellow Covenanters – least of all with Argyll. Making his way to the Highlands, he proceeded in the summer of 1644 to raise a force which consisted mainly of Highlanders, but also included a contingent of mercenaries and Scottish expatriates from Ireland and a few Royalist lairds from the Lowlands. At the head of this oddly assorted army, with no artillery and very little cavalry, he set out to win Scotland for the King, who in return made him a marquess.

Advancing in September on Perth, he utterly defeated a much larger force of Covenanters under Lord Elcho at Tippermuir and captured the city. Lord Elcho's troops, who had been assured that the Holy Ghost had promised them victory and advanced into battle to the incongruous cry of 'Jesus and no quarter', now fled in confusion. A couple of weeks later Montrose entered Aberdeen, a rich prey for the hungry Highlanders, who on this occasion seem to have conducted themselves with less than their usual chivalry, while the Irish contingent murdered and looted with characteristic gusto. He next turned westwards through the hills into Campbell country, and, with the ready help of the Macleans and the Macdonalds, always glad of an opportunity to pay off old scores and ready to sink their own differences in such a good cause, swooped on

Argyll's stronghold of Inveraray, burning it to the ground and causing its noble occupant to rise abruptly from his dinner-table and take refuge in a boat in the middle of Loch Fyne. In February 1645 Montrose won yet another victory at Inverlochy, when, after an arduous march through the snowy hills, he once more routed the Campbells and their Covenanting allies and again forced their Chief to leave his followers to their fate and make off by boat. 'I have traversed all the north of Scotland up to Argyle's country,' he wrote to Charles next day, 'who durst not stay my coming, or I should have given your Majesty a good account of him ere now. But at last I have met with him, yesterday, to his cost. . . . I departed out of Argyleshire, and marched through Lorn, Glencow and Lochaber, till I came to Loch Ness, my design being to fall upon Argyle before Seaforth and the Frasers could join him. My march was through inaccessible mountains. . . . I was willing to let the world see that Argyle was not the man his Highlandmen believed him to be, and that it was possible to beat him in his own Highlands.' Continuing his triumphant progress, Montrose went on in March to storm the walled city of Dundee; in May he smashed the Covenanters at Auldearn near the Moray Firth; in July he routed them at Alford outside Aberdeen; finally in August he again defeated them at Kilsyth and occupied Glasgow.

Montrose and his Highland allies had covered themselves with military glory. But they had so far failed to win the support of the Lowlands or for that matter to relieve Cromwell's pressure on the King's forces in England. In June 1645, at the height of Montrose's victorious progress through Scotland, the Royalist forces in England had suffered a disastrous defeat at Naseby. In September David Leslie, returning from England with a Covenanting force of four thousand seasoned troops, surprised, out-generalled and heavily defeated Montrose at Philiphaugh.

It was Montrose's first defeat. During the months that followed he still hoped to restore the King's fortunes in Scotland. Then in May 1646 came the news that Charles had surrendered to the Scottish army at Newark in England and that it had been made a condition of his surrender that Montrose should disband his followers and leave Scotland. Disillusioned and depressed, he took ship to Norway.

The Scots in England now found themselves in some perplexity. Their primary purpose in signing the Solemn League and Covenant with the English Parliament had been to secure England's conversion to Presbyterianism. They were only indirectly concerned with the quarrel between King and Parliament.

THE DESCRIPTION OF T[HE]

S[r] Tomas Fairefax his Excelle[nce]

NASBYE

Disposition of the opposing forces at the Battle of Naseby, June 1645. The Royalist forces are at the top of the picture, with 'the King's Majesty' at the centre.

OF HORSE AND FOOT OF HIS MAJESTIES, AND
drawn into severall bodyes, at the *Battayle* at *NASBYE*
werteenth day of *June* 1645

But it was growing ever clearer that, despite the Solemn League and Covenant and despite the deliberations of the Westminster Assembly, the establishment of Presbyterianism in England was becoming an increasingly remote possibility. Power in England was passing more and more into the hands of the Army and of its master, Oliver Cromwell. And neither Cromwell nor his Army were at all interested in turning England Presbyterian. Nor, despite the valuable services they had rendered, had the Scots received the monthly payments due to them under the agreement. Had the King declared his readiness to establish the Presbyterian religion in England, they would have been prepared at this stage to change sides and fight for him. But this the King declined to do. And so in return for a promise of £400,000, they handed him over to the English Parliamentary Commissioners and went back to Scotland. 'Traitor Scot', jeered the English, 'sold his King for a groat.' But the Covenanters, for their part, indignantly rejected the suggestion that they had behaved in any way dishonourably.

No sooner had the Scots handed over King Charles, than they began, rather characteristically, to have doubts about the wisdom of their action. They wondered, in particular, whether the English Parliament might not now seek to diminish the King's authority and whether things might not after all have been better otherwise. They accordingly sent secret emissaries, among them the wily Earl of Lauderdale, to resume contact with Charles, now more or less a prisoner in the Isle of Wight, and also to sound him out once again about the topic that was ever uppermost in their minds.

The result of these soundings was an agreement, arrived at towards the end of 1647 between the King and the representatives of the Scottish Parliament and styled the Engagement, under which the Scottish signatories, who became known as the Engagers, undertook to send an army to England to support the King in return for a promise from the latter to give Presbyterianism a three years' trial in England.

And indeed in the summer of 1648 a Scottish army, commanded by the Duke of Hamilton, actually set out for England to restore the King's position. It reached Preston in Lancashire, where it was heavily defeated by Cromwell and Hamilton himself captured and executed. What remained of the army surrendered, without having done anything to improve its own or the King's position.

The Engagement had always been strongly opposed by the more extreme Covenanters, the anti-Engagers or Whigs, as they were known. Taking the disaster of Preston as their cue, they now marched on Edinburgh from the south-west, where their strength lay, and overthrew the Government. This left their leader Argyll to all intents and purposes master of Scotland. Under Argyll's auspices, Cromwell now came to Edinburgh and there received a hero's welcome. Before leaving, he let it be known that he did not wish anyone who had fought for King Charles to hold any office in Scotland. In January the Scottish Parliament obediently gave effect to his wishes by passing a measure known as the Act of Classes. A few days later news reached Scotland that the King had been executed in Whitehall.

The news of the King's execution by the English was received in Scotland with dismay. Even Argyll is said to have been disturbed by it and Montrose, when he heard of it in exile in Brussels, fainted from the shock. To all sections of opinion, even those most strongly opposed to Charles's policies, it seemed

Execution of Charles I in Whitehall, January 1649. One of the onlookers, like Montrose when he heard of it, has fainted away.

unbecoming that Scotland, through English action, should be left without a king. Accordingly Argyll now established contact with the dead King's eighteen-year-old heir, Prince Charles, and, as a first step, had him proclaimed King in Edinburgh.

Montrose meanwhile had also offered the new King his services and had received from him the assignment of invading on his behalf the north of Scotland. The enterprise was ill-fated from the outset. Crossing to Orkney and thence to Thurso, Montrose assembled a mixed force of foreign mercenaries, Orcadians and local recruits. This was easily dispersed at Carbisdale in Ross-shire and Montrose himself handed over to his enemies by Macleod of Assynt, 'ane of his auld acquentance', who was awarded for this service £25,000 Scots. An eyewitness from the enemy camp, the Reverend James Fraser, later chaplain to the Covenanting Lord Lovat, has described how he was brought to Beauly as a prisoner, 'upon a little shelty horse, his feet fastened under the horse's belly with a tether and a bit halter for a bridle. . . . Yet, with a majesty and a state becoming him, kept his countenance high.'

At the instance of Argyll Montrose was now taken to Edinburgh, put on trial as a traitor to the King he had served so loyally, and in May 1649 hanged and quartered. He met his unpleasant fate with a calm dignity which won the respect even of the Edinburgh mob who had flocked in their thousands to watch him die. 'I never saw', wrote an Englishman in the crowd, 'a more sweeter carriage in a man in my life. I should write more largely if I had time: but he is just now a-turning off from the ladder; but his countenance changes not.' Of Argyll it is recorded that, as the cart bearing Montrose approached his house, he turned away from the balcony on which he had been standing and went indoors.

With Montrose gone, Charles II became entirely dependent on Argyll and bound, if he wanted to come to Scotland as King, to comply with the latter's wishes. The strongest pressure was brought to bear and in the end the young man agreed, though doubtless with certain mental reservations, to accept both Covenants and in the summer of 1650 arrived in Scotland to claim his Kingdom.

Cromwell's answer was at once to invade Scotland. At Dunbar he out-manœuvred and utterly routed a Scottish army under his former ally, General David Leslie. 'The Lord', was his pious comment when he saw the relative positions of the two forces, 'hath delivered them into our hands.' He then occupied Edinburgh.

But Cromwell's failure to fulfil the terms of the Solemn League and Covenant still rankled and the Covenanters were still reluctant to deal with him. Even

A contemporary Dutch broadsheet shows Charles II (*centre, right*) crowned by the Marquess of Argyll. In the foreground, the King is being girded for war by Ireland, while Scotland hands him a pistol labelled 'Revenge'. Douglas, in Puritan garb, preaches on the text 'Let us swallow them up alive' (Proverbs 1: 12).

now they would not admit defeat. On New Year's Day 1651 Charles II was crowned King by Argyll at Scone and, in spite of opposition from the more extreme Covenanters, the Act of Classes was formally repealed. Men who had fought for Charles I were now no longer debarred from fighting for his son and by the summer of 1651 David Leslie had assembled a sizeable army with which to guard the approaches to Stirling.

But again disaster overtook the Scots. At Inverkeithing, near North Queensferry, a Scottish force composed of both Highlanders and Lowlanders, thrown in to check Cromwell's progress northwards, found themselves heavily outnumbered by an English army under General Lambert. The bulk of the Lowland cavalry under Holborn of Menstrie turned and fled. The Highlanders, mainly Macleans, stood and fought. Of eight hundred Maclean clansmen who took the field under Hector Maclean of Duart, seven hundred and sixty were killed, including Duart himself and two of the sons of Maclean of Ardgour. 'Another for Hector' the clansmen are said to have cried as they died beside their Chief. It was rumoured afterwards that Argyll, for reasons of his own, had ensured that no reinforcements should reach them. However this may be, the way was now open to Cromwell, who marched on Perth and soon controlled the country both to the north and to the south of the Forth.

Outmanœuvred in Scotland, Leslie and his main force next crossed the Border into England in the hope of winning more support there. It was a bold move, but it failed. Leaving General Monck to deal with Scotland, Cromwell himself followed the Scottish army into England, picking up reinforcements on the way. On 3 September 1651 the two armies met at Worcester and there, on the banks of the Severn, the third army the Scots had raised in as many years was heavily defeated and driven to surrender. 'The Crowning Mercy', Cromwell called it.

Among the few who eluded capture was King Charles himself, who, after various adventures, managed to make his way to the Continent, and now, in his own words 'went on his travels'. A few days earlier Monck's troops had captured the Committee of the Estates, which was all that was left of the Scottish Parliament, and had also stormed the rich city of Dundee. Scottish resistance was to all intents and purposes at an end.

A satirical English view of the relationship between Charles II and his Presbyterian Scottish subjects. The Presbyter holds the King's nose to the grindstone, but the King, under his breath, expresses mental reservations.

Chapter Five

'ANE END OF ANE AULD SANG'

Cromwell, now Lord Protector, spent the next year or so in stamping out such vestiges of resistance as remained and setting up in Scotland an efficient system of military government with English garrisons in the principal towns and strongpoints. Even the Highlands were temporarily subdued. In due course Scotland was formally united with England by a Treaty of Union and became part of Cromwell's Commonwealth. There were no further meetings of the Scottish Parliament, but thirty Scottish Members were sent to represent Scotland in the Commons at Westminster. In return for the loss of their independence the Scots received certain economic benefits. 'As for the embodying of Scotland with England,' wrote Robert Blair, 'it will be as when the poor bird is embodied with the hawk that hath eaten it up.'

The resulting regime was probably the most efficient and orderly the country had ever experienced. 'A man', it was claimed, 'could ride all over Scotland with a switch in his hand and £100 in his pocket, which he could not have done these 500 years.' It was also, like so many efficient regimes, deeply unpopular. The English, oddly enough, were unable to understand the reasons for their own unpopularity. 'Soe senceless', wrote one of them, 'are this generation of theire owne goode that scarce a man of them showed any sign of rejoycing.'

Prominent among the few Scots who came to terms with Cromwell was Argyll, 'that political lord', who, despite his support of Charles II in 1649, managed, with characteristic flexibility, to make himself acceptable to his successors. His luck changed, however, when in 1660, after Cromwell's death and the collapse of the Protectorate in England, Charles at General Monck's behest returned from exile and resumed his throne. Then, like his enemy Montrose a dozen years earlier, Argyll in his turn was, to his pained surprise,

Great Seal of England, 1651, showing Parliament in session, with thirty Scottish representatives.

Restoration

133

Charles II, 'whose word no man relies on', signed the two Covenants in 1649, but considered Presbytery 'not a religion for gentlemen'. Red chalk drawing by Pieter van der Banck.

arraigned for treason and duly executed, though in a less barbarous manner than his rival. He, too, to give him his due, met his end with dignity and composure. 'I set the crown on the King's head,' he said. 'He hastens me now to a better crown than his.' After his execution his severed head was set on the same spike in the Tolbooth from which Montrose's had only lately been removed.

Charles II, for his part, was never again to visit Scotland. For the next twenty-five years, like his father and grandfather before him, he governed his northern kingdom through a Privy Council situated in Edinburgh and a Secretary based in London. The latter appointment was, for a start, entrusted to the Earl (later Duke) of Lauderdale, who in the last reign had been a dedicated Covenanter, but had since come to hold other views. For most of Charles's reign, as Secretary and later as Commissioner, it was he who governed Scotland.

Charles, who considered that 'Presbytery was not a religion for gentlemen' and had only signed the two Covenants in 1649 in order to secure his own coronation, had no intention of carrying out the political and religious obligations he had at that time undertaken or, for that matter, those undertaken by his father before him. He chose his Privy Council and his Officers of State without reference to Parliament, and the Scottish Parliament, when it met in 1661, was packed with reliable Royalists who lost no time in rescinding most of the measures passed since 1633. This meant, first and foremost, the restoration of James VI's method of himself choosing the Committee of Articles, which further greatly strengthened the King's position in relation to Parliament. It also had the effect, as far as the Church was concerned, of bringing back bishops and restoring the former system of patronage, under which ministers were chosen by the laird and not by the congregation. As for James Sharp, a Covenanting minister, who had been sent to London from Scotland to make representations at Court as the emissary of the moderate Presbyterians, he came back Archbishop of St Andrews and professing entirely different opinions from those with which he had set out.

Under the new regulations, ministers appointed since 1649 were required to resign their charges and receive them again from their bishops and patrons. No significant changes were made in doctrine or in the order of worship and most ministers in the end agreed to the new procedure. But some three hundred, or about a third of the total number, refused to do so and left their manses and

The Covenanters

View of the Parliament House and Exchequer, Edinburgh.

Silver quaich, traditional Scottish drinking-vessel. Engraved lines echo the barrel-stave construction of older versions in wood.

their churches rather than submit. What is more, they had, particularly in the south-west, the support of their parishioners, people of no great account, maybe, but of great steadfastness. And before long unauthorized religious services were being held in many areas by these 'outed ministers' in houses and barns and on the bare hillside.

As time went on, the Privy Council reacted with increasing severity to this open defiance of the law, while the former Covenanter Lauderdale, for his part, wished that there might be a regular rebellion, 'that so I might bring over an army of Irish Papists to cut all their throats'. Troops were sent to collect fines from those attending illegal conventicles, and armed clashes ensued. But this did not dismay the Covenanters who, as good Calvinists, knew that they were pre-destined to grace and so were the more eager to die for their faith. In spite of the savage punishments inflicted on them, their resistance continued unabated and as often as not they gave the Government forces as good as they got. Thus in 1679 the promising career of the unfortunate Archbishop Sharp was brought to an

Murder of Archbishop Sharp of St Andrews. In 1679 he was dragged from his coach and slain by a party of Covenanters, who claimed to have 'received a call from God' to punish the former Covenanting minister.

The Battle of Drumclog, 1679. On a boggy moor on the borders of Ayrshire and Lanarkshire, the Covenanters, forty horse and two hundred foot, routed a stronger Government force under Graham of Claverhouse.

end when he was dragged from his coach and brutally murdered by a party of Covenanters who claimed that they had 'received a call from God to put him to death', while not long after three troops of Government horse under Graham of Claverhouse were utterly routed by a rabble of armed Covenanters.

The Government now reacted more vigorously than ever. A strong force under the King's illegitimate son, James Duke of Monmouth, was sent to deal with the rebels and at Bothwell Brig the Covenanters were heavily defeated and fourteen hundred prisoners herded into Greyfriars churchyard in Edinburgh to await their various unpleasant ends. But the resistance of the Covenanters continued as stubborn as ever, while the Government's measures of repression grew increasingly severe. At the market cross in Sanquhar the preacher Richard Cameron publicly called his followers to armed insurrection against the King and his Government. He and those who listened to him met with the fate that was to be expected. It was not for nothing that the 1680's became known as the Killing Time.

137

James VII and II, as Duke of York: portrait by Sir Peter Lely. When his brother, Charles II, died Scotland had a Catholic King, the first for 120 years.

James VII

In 1685 Charles II died and was succeeded by his brother James VII, who towards the end of Charles's reign, during the Killing Time, had, as Duke of York, briefly acted as Royal Commissioner in Scotland. He was popular neither in the Lowlands of Scotland nor in England. For the first time for nearly a hundred and twenty years Scotland had a Roman Catholic monarch and his subjects, both in Scotland and England, not unnaturally suspected him of wanting to establish his own religion throughout his dominions. Nor, in that age of intolerance, did he in any way endear himself to most of them by using the royal prerogative to accord complete toleration to all his subjects, Roman

Signatures of King Charles II, as Founder of the Royal Society, and his brother, as an Honorary Fellow.

Opposite: Part of a despatch to the Earl of Linlithgow from Graham of Claverhouse, describing the rout at Drumclog. He ends, 'My Lord, I am so wearied and so sleapy that I have wryten this very confusedly'.

Catholics, Covenanters and Quakers alike. Under Charles, opposition to the King's policy had been largely local and had come in the main from the lower orders. Under James it was more broadly based. It was also actively encouraged from Holland by James's Dutch son-in-law, William of Orange, a devious, unscrupulous man, who himself had designs on his father-in-law's throne. Attempted insurrections, under Argyll in Scotland and Monmouth in England, were unsuccessful, but in November 1688, at the invitation of the Whig leaders, William of Orange landed in England with an army. James, after much vacillation, fled to France and in February 1689 his son-in-law William and daughter Mary were proclaimed King and Queen of England and Ireland. In Scotland a Convention of Estates, which had been summoned after various preliminary soundings to decide what should be done, showed a majority for William and Mary and in April 1689 they were accordingly also proclaimed King and Queen of Scotland. As at the Restoration so now Scotland had simply followed England's example.

Dutch William

There were those, however, in the Highlands who still remained true to their legitimate monarch, greatly preferring him to a Dutch usurper. They were known as Jacobites. When William was proclaimed King, Graham of Claverhouse, now Viscount Dundee, rode north to raise the loyal clans for King James who had himself now landed in Ireland. A body of troops under General Hugh Mackay was sent by William to put down the Highland Jacobites. At sundown on 27 July 1689, at the head of the narrow gorge of Killiecrankie in Perthshire, the Highlanders fell upon William's soldiers 'like madmen' and almost annihilated them. But Dundee himself was killed in the battle and his troops were left without a leader. And so, after another savage encounter with the Government troops in the churchyard at Dunkeld, in which the dour followers of Richard Cameron, now formed into a regiment and known as the Cameronians, distinguished themselves by the doggedness of their defence, the Highlanders in the end faded ineffectually back into their hills and glens and left the field to their

John Graham of Claverhouse, Viscount Dundee.

Scottish dragoon of 1680, under the command of Viscount Dundee.

View of the town of Dunkeld, 1693. Here after a dogged defence by the Cameronians, the Jacobite resistance to Dutch William effectively came to an end.

The town and abbey of Dunfermline in the time of William and Mary.

Siege of Londonderry in 1689 by James VII; the Battle of the Boyne ended his hopes of returning to the throne by way of Ireland.

enemies. A fresh Jacobite attempt in the spring ended in disaster at Cromdale on Speyside and six weeks later the Battle of the Boyne put an end to James's Irish campaign and caused him finally to withdraw to France.

Despite the setbacks suffered by the Jacobites, Dutch William's Government and in particular his Secretary of State, Sir John Dalrymple, the Master of Stair, were still uneasy about the Highlands and sought anxiously for a means of enforcing their will there. As a first step they sent General Mackay to build and garrison a strongpoint near Inverlochy to be named Fort William. At the same time the sum of £12,000 was entrusted to Iain Glas or Grey John, the Campbell Earl of Breadalbane, an equivocal figure of doubtful loyalty to anyone – 'cunning as a fox, slippery as an eel', was the verdict of a contemporary. This money was to be distributed among the chiefs in the hope of making them loyal to William. Some accepted the bribe; others refused it. But none became any more loyal to William than they had been before.

The Government now decided to adopt other tactics. They were character-istic of the personalities involved. 'There never was trouble brewing in Scotland,' Charles II had once said, 'but that a Dalrymple or a Campbell was at the bottom of it.' This time the honours were shared between them. 'I think,' wrote Stair to Breadalbane, 'the Clan Donell must be rooted out and Lochiel. Leave the McLeans to Argyll. . . . God knows whether the £12,000 sterling had been better employed to settle the Highlands or to ravage them: but since we will make them desperate, I think we should root them out before they can get the help they depend upon.' 'Look on', he wrote to the same correspondent next day, 'and you shall be gratified of your revenge.' Seldom has the hereditary hatred of the Lowlander for the Highlander – *mi-run mor nan Gall* – found more vigorous expression.

The Government now issued a proclamation ordering the chiefs of the various clans to take the oath of allegiance to King William not later than 1 January 1692. Failing this, recourse would be had to fire and sword. The time of year was carefully chosen. 'The winter time', wrote Stair, 'is the only season in which we are sure the Highlanders cannot escape, and carry their wives, bairns and cattle to the hills. . . . This is the proper time to maul them in the long dark nights.'

But the mauling was not to be on the scale that the Master had hoped for. From his exile in France King James at the last moment authorized the chiefs to swear allegiance to his Dutch son-in-law. Stair was sadly disappointed. By the appointed date only two chiefs had failed to take the oath, the powerful MacDonell of Glengarry and the elderly chieftain of a minor, but notoriously turbulent, sept of the MacDonalds, MacIan MacDonald of Glencoe. The latter, partly from dilatoriness and partly through the inclemency of the weather, arrived three days late in Inveraray, the seat of the Sheriff-depute, where, owing to the absence of that officer, he was only able to take the oath on 6 January.

This gave William the opportunity for which he and his advisers were

John Campbell, Earl of
Breadalbane: portrait by
Sir John Medina.

143

Captain Robert Campbell of Glenlyon. He commanded the Government troops in the massacre of Glencoe.

Opposite: The order, signed by Major Duncanson, to Campbell of Glenlyon, 'for the good and safty of the Country, that those miscreants be cutt off root and branch'.

looking. At the instance of his Secretary of State, he allowed the powerful Glengarry another chance. MacIan he picked as his victim. 'If MacIan of Glencoe and that tribe', he wrote to the General commanding his troops in the Highlands, 'can be well separated from the rest, it will be a proper vindication of public justice to extirpate that sect of thieves.'

And so a company of trustworthy Campbell troops, from the Earl of Argyll's Regiment of Foot, commanded, as it happened, by a relative by marriage of MacIan's, Captain Robert Campbell of Glenlyon, were sent to Glencoe and billeted in the cottages of the clansmen. The MacDonalds received them hospitably. Captain Campbell spent a couple of weeks drinking and playing cards with MacIan and his sons, while his soldiers fraternized with the clansmen. Then, on 12 February, he received from his military superior, Major Duncanson, the following instructions: 'You are hereby ordered to fall upon the McDonalds of Glencoe and put all to the sword under seventy; you are to have a special care that the old fox and his sons doe on no account escape your hands.'

That night Robert Campbell and two of his officers accepted an invitation to dine with MacIan. Meanwhile a force of four hundred Government troops moved to block the northern approach to the glen and four hundred more to close the southern. At five in the morning of 13 February Glenlyon and his troops started to carry out their instructions. Parties of soldiers went from cottage to cottage, slaughtering the sleeping MacDonalds and setting light to their

You are hereby ordered to fall upon the Rebells, the McDonalds of Glenco, and putt all to the sword under seventy. you are to have a speciall care that the old Fox and his sones doe upon no account escape your hands, you are to secure all the avenues that no man escape. This you are to putt in execution att fyve of the clock precisely; and by that time, or verie shortly after it, I'le strive to be att you with a stronger party: if I doe not come to you att fyve, you are not to tary for me, butt to fall on. This is by the Kings speciall command, for the good & safty of the Country, that these miscreants be cutt off root and branch. See that this be putt in execution without feud or favour, else you may expect to be dealt with as one not true to King nor Goverment, nor a man fitt to carry Commission in the Kings service. Expecting you will not faill in the fulfilling hereof, as you love your selfe, I subscribe these with my hand att Balicholis feb: 12, 1692

for thir Maties service.

To Capt
Robert Campbell
of Glenlyon.

The Pass of Glencoe.

houses. MacIan himself was shot by one of his guests of the night before. A Campbell soldier gnawed the rings from Lady Glencoe's fingers with his teeth. A child of six, who clung, begging for mercy, to Glenlyon's knees, was promptly dispatched. As the massacre proceeded, snow began to fall. Some of the inhabitants of the glen were able to escape in the confusion. Others died in the snow.

King William and Stair had succeeded in their object, which was to make an example of a Jacobite clan and establish a measure of control over the Highlands. But, in spite of their efforts to hush things up, the affair gave rise to unfavourable comment, not only in the Highlands, but in the Lowlands and even in England, and in the end William was forced to dispense with the services of his Secretary of State. In due course, however, Stair was rewarded with an earldom, while Campbell of Glenlyon was promoted to colonel. King William, for his part, despite documentary evidence to the contrary, loftily disclaimed any previous knowledge of the affair.

In Church matters, too, the new King, though reassuringly Protestant, found himself confronted with a number of problems. Most Scottish Episcopalians were opposed to him on dynastic grounds, while many Presbyterians suspected him of being half-hearted in his attitude towards 'prelacy'. A settlement had finally been reached in 1690 under which bishops and patronage were abolished, the Westminster Confession re-adopted, Episcopalian ministers driven out and the Presbyterian system re-established in its entirety. But William's not unreasonable plan for a wider and more comprehensive solution was doomed to failure.

Nor did William's reign do much in other ways to improve feeling between Scotland and England. The massacre of Glencoe, while doubtless winning him the admiration of the Whigs, had sullied his reputation in the Highlands. Soon disillusionment with the Dutch monarch and his London-based advisers was to spread to the commercially minded Lowlands as well. And for very good reason.

Highland Chieftain of the 1660's.

Under the English Navigation Act, goods could only be imported into English ports in English ships or in ships belonging to their country of origin. This was a serious obstacle to the expansion of Scottish overseas trade. So were the virtual monopolies established by the English East India and Africa Companies. At every turn the Scottish trader found his way blocked by privileged English competitors.

In June 1695 a project was launched, designed to redress the balance and give Scottish merchants a better chance. At the instance of an enterprising operator from Dumfriesshire named William Paterson, who amongst other things had helped to found the Bank of England and to give North London its efficient new water supply, an Act was passed by the Scottish Parliament establishing The Company of Scotland Trading to Africa and the Indies. The capital of the new Company was to be £600,000 of which half was to be subscribed in Scotland and the rest in England and elsewhere. And one of its first aims was to gain control of what Paterson called 'the Door of the Seas, the Key of the Universe', namely the narrow isthmus of Darien, linking North and South America. Here goods for India could be transhipped and replaced by goods

The Darien Scheme

147

Map of 'The Isthmus of Darian', or New Caledonia.

from India, and the long journey round the Cape of Good Hope or Cape Horn thus avoided. It would also give Scotland something she had lacked since Charles I had sold Nova Scotia to the French within a dozen years of its foundation, namely a colony of her own.

The necessary £300,000 had soon been subscribed in London and good progress was being made when it became known that King William personally disapproved of the project. At this stage the English subscribers hastily withdrew and Paterson was left to find the balance of his capital elsewhere. He turned to Holland and Hamburg; but here too William brought pressure to bear. In the end the scheme was launched with a capital of some £400,000, almost entirely subscribed in Scotland and representing a high proportion of the nation's cash resources. And in July 1698 Paterson and three ships with 1,200 emigrants on board set sail from the Port of Leith for Darien, or New Caledonia, as the proposed colony was to be called. The colonists carried with them a cargo including 4,000 periwigs, some bobwigs and blue bonnets and a great many Bibles, as well as large quantities of serge, huckabacks and gridirons. They seem to have had no knowledge of the climate of the Isthmus or of its malarial marshes. Nor do they appear to have realized that it belonged in fact to the King of Spain, with whom King William was at this moment seeking to conclude an alliance.

Paterson and his party reached Darien in November. Without waiting to hear how the first expedition had fared, a second and then a third group of settlers set out. By the summer of 1699 pestilence had killed a quarter of the members of the original expedition. The remainder, as a result of inadequate provisioning, faced starvation. On appealing to the English colony of Jamaica for provisions, they were told that King William had expressly forbidden his colonial officials to help them in any way. There were rumours, too, of an impending Spanish attack. No trade had been done at all. In July 1699 Paterson himself and the fever-stricken survivors of the ill-fated first expedition finally set sail for home. Long before they reached their destination almost half had died of the fever they carried on them.

It was thus that when the second Darien expedition arrived a few weeks later, they found the bravely named Fort St Andrew abandoned and just enough survivors still left to tell them of the disaster that had overtaken them. They themselves stayed long enough to catch the prevailing pestilence and to lose one of their two ships by fire as she lay at anchor. Then they too left, huddled

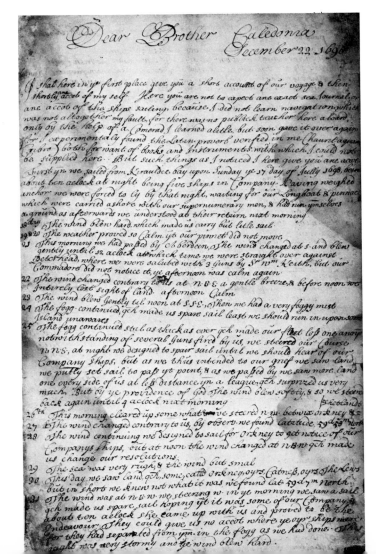

This letter from Colin Campbell to his brother is the only surviving first-hand account of the Darien fiasco. 'Five ships in Company' set sail 'upon Sunday ye 17 day of Jully 1698'. By 22nd December, the date of this letter, disaster had overtaken the colonists.

in a single ship – *The Hopeful Binning of Bo'ness*. By the time they reached the inhospitable shores of Jamaica, nearly half their number had died of fever.

Meanwhile, at the end of September 1699, a third expedition had set out with another 1,300 prospective settlers. Fever was not their only problem. They had barely had time to man the defences of Fort St Andrew before the Spaniards attacked them in strength from land and sea. After stubbornly defending themselves for more than a month, they finally surrendered. The Spaniards were so impressed by their courage that they allowed those of them who could still stand to march out with flags flying and drums beating. But they insisted that they should leave Darien. And once again the journey back brought more deaths and the loss of another ship.

The Darien Scheme had been a disaster. Two thousand Scottish lives and three hundred thousand Scottish pounds had been lost. And the responsibility, as far as Scotland was concerned, lay fairly and squarely with William of Orange and the English. By the time William died in March 1702 and was succeeded by his sister-in-law Anne, hatred for England had reached new heights and in the months that followed, a number of other deplorable incidents still further exacerbated relations between the two countries.

Such was the background against which, from both sides, feelers were now surprisingly enough put out for union between the two countries. At first sight the prospects of success could not have seemed less favourable. But to many Scots it had by now begun to appear that their country's only hope of economic survival lay in some kind of deal with their southern neighbours, which would admit them to the trading privileges at present exclusively enjoyed by the English and which the English were at present most reluctant to share. Nor did such a deal need to be entirely one-sided. The Scots, as it happened, possessed one important bargaining counter.

Queen Anne, who had succeeded to both thrones on her brother-in-law's death, had given birth at one time or another to seventeen children, but the last survivor of these, the little Duke of Gloucester, had died two years earlier. She therefore had no direct heir.

The Whig statesmen now in power in England feared nothing more than the possibility of a second Stuart restoration. For one thing, England was predominantly Protestant, while James Edward, the son of James VII and II, who since his father's death in 1701 was legally King, was, unlike his two half-sisters, Mary and Anne, a Roman Catholic. The Whigs were also profoundly opposed to the Stuart concept of the monarchy, which did not at all correspond to their own ideas. In 1701 an Act of Settlement had accordingly been passed through the English Parliament, designed to ensure that on Anne's death the English Crown should go, not to James Edward, but to a German princess, the Electress Sophia of Hanover, granddaughter, through the female line, of James VI and I. Having achieved this, it now remained for the Whigs to make certain that 'the backdoor' as the Bishop of Salisbury put it, should be 'shut against the attempts of the Pretender Prince of Wales', in other words that, independently of what happened in England, there should be no Stuart restoration in Scotland. Which, so long as Scotland remained a separate country, was always a possibility.

The potentialities of this situation were not lost on the Scots. In 1704 the Scottish Parliament passed by a substantial majority an Act of Security. This *Act of Security* provided that Parliament should name the successor to the throne of Scotland within twenty days of the death of the reigning sovereign. This successor was to be a Protestant and a descendant of the House of Stuart, but was not to be the occupant of the throne of England, unless Scotland were given equal trading rights and liberty in government and religion. It also provided, rather pointedly, for a military force to be trained for the defence of the country. Further measures removed foreign policy from the control of the Sovereign and provided for the duty-free import of French wines. These measures acquired added significance from the fact that England was now at war with France.

Queen Anne's Whig ministers at first advised her to withhold her consent from the Act of Security, which needless to say, had aroused great indignation in England, but in the end agreed that she should grant it for fear that otherwise

The birth of a son, James Edward, to the Catholic King James VII and II in 1688. The baby is held, and presumably blessed, by the Papal Nuncio.

the Scots might retaliate by allowing French warships to use Scottish ports. In March 1705, however, the English Parliament responded with the Aliens Act. Under this all Scotsmen were to be treated as aliens, especially for trading purposes, unless Scotland accepted the Hanoverian succession by Christmas.

Within a month tension between the two countries was further heightened by the execution on Leith sands, at the behest of the Edinburgh mob, of an English sea-captain called Green and two of his crew, accused, wrongly as it happened, of having piratically seized the Scottish ship *Speedy Return* somewhere off the Malabar coast. The execution took place despite urgent entreaties from Queen Anne and in the teeth of all the available evidence. But such considerations weighed less with the Scottish Privy Council than did the menaces of the Edinburgh mob. The two countries now seemed close to war.

But the English Government, already at war with France, did not want war with Scotland as well. The alternative was some sort of accommodation. And so in the summer of 1705 the young Duke of Argyll, who had distinguished himself fighting for the English under Marlborough in the Low Countries and whose family and clan were not handicapped by a record of undue loyalty to the Stuart cause, was dispatched to Edinburgh as the Queen's Commissioner, with the task of persuading the Scottish Parliament to authorize negotiations for a Treaty of Union. After some weeks of acrimonious debate Parliament finally gave their consent and in April 1706 thirty-one Scottish Commissioners, for the most part sound Whigs, and including the newly created Earl of Stair, were sent off to London to open negotiations with an equal number of English Commissioners.

In the negotiations that followed, the Scottish Commissioners sought to retain Scotland's national Parliament, in other words to make the proposed union a federal one. But the English rejected a federal solution from the start, insisting that the Scots must pay a higher price for commercial equality with England. In the end it was agreed that there should be a combined British Parliament to which Scotland should contribute sixteen representative Peers and only forty-five Members of the House of Commons as against more than five hundred English Members. It was also agreed that Scotland should bind herself to accept the Hanoverian succession. In return the Scots would receive 'full freedom and intercourse of trade and navigation'. Financially, Scotland was to be awarded the sum of £398,085 10s 0d, to be known as the Equivalent, partly in return for taking over a share of the English National Debt and partly as compensation to the shareholders in the Darien Company. Finally the Scot

John Campbell, second Duke of Argyll. As Queen Anne's Commissioner he persuaded the Scottish Parliament to enter into negotiations for a Treaty of Union between the two countries.

were to retain their own legal system and the special rights of the Royal Burghs. On all flags the emblems of both countries were to be united.

Such, in its main outlines, was the Treaty which was submitted to the Scottish Parliament when it met in October 1706. To allay Presbyterian fears that an English-controlled Parliament might saddle Scotland with an Anglican Church, a Bill of Security had been drafted, affirming that the Church was 'to continue without any alteration with the people of this land in all succeeding generations'.

Even so it seemed on the face of it improbable that the Treaty would gain acceptance. In Parliament the Country Party, who opposed it, outnumbered the Court Party, who were in favour of acceptance. Outside Parliament, public opinion was thoroughly hostile. Mob violence and agitation against the Treaty threatened at any moment to develop into open insurrection. The Duke of Queensberry, now High Commissioner, was chased down the Canongate to Holyrood by an angry crowd who stoned his coach. 'His Grace', we are told, 'was constantly saluted with curses and imprecations as he passed through the streets, and if Parliament sat till towards evening, he and his guards were all well pelted with stones . . . so that often he and his retinue were obliged to go off at a top gallop and in great disorder.' The Duke of Hamilton, on the other hand, who was believed to head the opposition to the Treaty, was cheered whenever he showed his face. In the end three regiments of soldiers had to be called in to keep order. In Glasgow things were even more out of control and the Provost was obliged to hide from the angry crowd in a folding bed. And further disorders broke out in other parts of the country.

But characteristically enough, the opponents of the Treaty, even at this critical juncture, were unable to agree among themselves or to act in unison. The Jacobites, for their part, totally rejected the Treaty and Lord Belhaven spoke movingly of 'our ancient Mother Caledonia . . . sitting in the midst of our Senate waiting for her own children to deal the fatal blow'. But when the time for voting arrived, an important section of the opposition, the so-called *Squadrone Volante*, at the last moment decided to vote with the Government, while the Duke of Hamilton, who had proclaimed his intention of staging a mass walk-out by the opposition, found, when it came to the point, that he was suffering from toothache and could not be present.

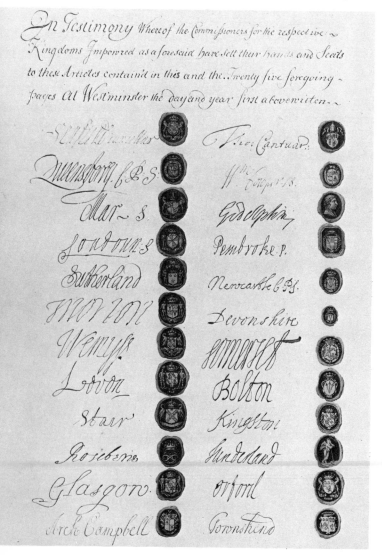

Signatures and seals of the Commissioners who negotiated the Treaty of Union, 22nd July 1706. The Scots signed on the left, the English (headed by the Archbishop of Canterbury) on the right.

The Duke of Queensberry, on behalf of Scotland, presenting the Treaty of Union to Queen Anne.

And so, while the mob roared outside and rumours of insurrection were rife, article by article the Treaty became law, reaching its final stages in January 1707 after the Act of Security had duly been incorporated in it. From all sides petitions against the Union poured in, 'fit' in Argyll's telling phrase, 'to make kites'. Meanwhile, from south of the Border came the news that Argyll's former comrade at arms and commander, Marlborough, was moving his cavalry northwards in strength. And gradually the protests and disorders subsided.

In the English Parliament the Treaty met with no opposition and on 6 March received the Royal assent. On 25 March the Scottish Parliament met for the last time to conclude a few routine transactions. 'The public business of this session now being over,' said Queensberry in a final speech, 'it is full time to put an end to it.'

And so, in this rather humdrum manner, Scotland was deprived of her sovereignty. 'There's ane end', said Lord Seafield, the Lord Privy Seal, 'of ane auld sang.' The Crown, the Sword and the Sceptre were wrapped in linen and stowed away in a box in Edinburgh Castle, and the Duke of Queensberry rode in triumph into London, where he received a pension of £3,000 a year and an English dukedom. The toothache-stricken Duke of Hamilton, on the other hand, had to wait four years for his. 'We are bought and sold,' sang the Jacobites, 'for English gold.' And they were not far wrong.

Scotland's Parliament had existed as a democratic legislature for less than twenty years. It is arguable that, had it survived longer, the native genius of the Scottish people might have found in it a means of expression not to be vouch-safed to them at Westminster, where their representatives would perforce always be in a minority.

The Crown of Scotland, last used at a coronation when the Marquess of Argyll placed it on the head of Charles II on New Year's Day, 1651.

Chapter Six

Although many of those responsible for the Treaty of Union doubtless believed at the time that they were acting in Scotland's best interest and saving her, if not from war, at any rate from economic disaster, the Union was from the start unpopular. It soon became more so. 'I never', reported the English agent Daniel Defoe, 'saw a nation so universally wild. . . . It seems a perfect gangrene of the temper.'

The Whigs were now in control and, from the working of the new British Parliament, it soon became all too evident that the Union was not to be one of equal partners. Much of the trouble concerned fiscal matters. 'Have we not bought the Scots, and a right to tax them?' an English member inquired with characteristic forthrightness. And Scottish Members who objected were told that Scotland was 'now but a county of Britain' and that 'now she is subject to the sovereignty of England, she must be governed by English maxims and laws'. Over ecclesiastical questions, too, there were indications that, despite the Act of Security, the position of the Presbyterians was not as secure as they had hoped, so that they, too, began to entertain doubts about the Union. Soon, discontent with the Union permeated all classes and all parts of the country and when in 1713 a motion to repeal the Union was submitted to the House of Lords by Seafield and Argyll, who had both played such an important part in bringing it about, it was only defeated by four votes.

It was only natural that in these circumstances, the Jacobites, who since James VII's death in 1701 had regarded his son James Edward as the rightful King and hoped for his return on his half-sister Anne's death, if not sooner, should have felt encouraged. 'The Jacobites', wrote Parson Wodrow of Eastwood in 1710, 'are mighty uppish . . . they talk their King will be over, either by Act of Parliament or by invasion by August next.' 'They boast mighty,' he added acidly, 'which I hope will ruin their cause.' Already many of the Tory leaders and even some Whigs, in England as well as in Scotland, were in touch with James at his Court in France and when Anne fell ill in 1714, a Jacobite coup seemed likely. In the event, however, this was averted by swift action on the part of the Whig Administration. On Anne's death she was at once succeeded by George of Hanover, son of the Electress Sophia, who had narrowly predeceased her cousin, and on 5 August 1714 George was publicly proclaimed King in Edinburgh. The following night the Duchess of Argyll gave a great ball at Holyrood to celebrate the occasion.

Had James been prepared to turn Protestant or had he and his supporters shown greater initiative, there seems little doubt that he could now without much difficulty have become King. George I was not only personally unattractive, but took little interest in his new subjects and had nothing in common with them, not even language. Politically, he was a Party monarch, relying exclusively on the Whigs to whom he owed his throne and deliberately cold-shouldering the Tories. When, with James's permission, the Highland Chiefs generously sent him an address of acceptance, George promptly rejected it. It was scarcely the way to win their allegiance. Meanwhile, even in the Lowlands discontent with the Union was rife and there were many who drank to the health of 'The King over the Water'. For the new dynasty the outlook was far from healthy.

James Edward

When James VII had died in 1701, Louis XIV of France, then on the brink of war with England, had promised to help his son. And in March 1708, less than a year after the Union, a sizeable French fleet had escorted James Edward to within sight of the Scottish coast. But an encounter with vessels of the English fleet had deterred the French commander and, despite James's entreaties, for he did not lack personal courage, the expedition had returned to France without ever putting him ashore.

Now, seven years later, in 1715, there was again talk of a Jacobite rising. This time there was less hope of help from France. In 1713 the Treaty of Utrecht had put an end to hostilities between France and England and, on the death of Louis XIV two years later, power passed to the Regent d'Orléans who was still less disposed to give active help to the Jacobites. But James Edward, who was now twenty-seven and had spent nearly all his life in exile, decided to make the attempt notwithstanding. In the summer of 1715 he accordingly wrote from France to the Earl of Mar, with whom he had for some time past been in correspondence, calling on him to raise the Clans without further delay.

Prince James Edward, aged thirteen, in 1701. In that year his father died and he became, in Jacobite eyes, King James VIII and III.

View of Perth, from John Slezer's *Theatrum Scotiae* (1693). Lord Mar captured the town for King James in 'the Fifteen'.

Lord Mar, or Bobbing John, as he was known to his contemporaries, had been a supporter of Queensberry and one of the signatories of the Treaty of Union. At the beginning of the new reign he had hastened to declare himself the 'faithful and dutiful subject and servant' of King George. But he had been disappointed by the latter's cool response and had accordingly established contact with the exiled Court. On receiving James's letter, he disguised himself as a workman and, going down to the London docks, boarded a collier for Scotland. Arriving towards the middle of August, he first summoned his friends and neighbours to a great *tinchal* or hunting party on the Braes of Mar and there acquainted all concerned with what was afoot. Three weeks later, on 6 September, he publicly proclaimed James VIII and III as King and raised the old Scottish standard at Castletown in Braemar, when, to the dismay of the superstitious spectators, the ornamental golden ball on the flagpole suddenly

fell to the ground. At the same time Lord Mar publicly declared that the Union had been a blunder, by which Scotland's 'ancient liberties were delivered into the hands of the English'.

At first the rising prospered. No fewer than twelve thousand armed Jacobite clansmen rallied to the standard under their chiefs and many of the northern towns declared for King James. By mid-September Mar had without difficulty captured Perth and from this point of vantage issued a number of resounding proclamations. Between him and the English border there lay only two thousand government troops based on Stirling and commanded by the Duke of Argyll.

But, whatever his qualities as a politician, Mar was no kind of military leader. Having once captured Perth, he stayed there for week after week, missing the opportunity for swift action against an enemy who was outnumbered and

*Raising
the Clans*

161

unprepared. Elsewhere individual clans made independent sorties. The MacGregors tried unsuccessfully to storm Dumbarton Castle while the Macleans and some of the Macdonalds marched on the Campbell stronghold of Inveraray in an unsuccessful attempt to repeat their exploits of Montrose's day. But this time there was no Montrose; there was not even a Dundee. And, after some indecisive exchanges with Argyll's brother, Islay, they withdrew to Strathfillan.

At last, learning early in November that the border Jacobites were stirring (Kenmure on the Scottish side and Derwentwater and Forster on the English), Mar dispatched his most experienced commander, Mackintosh of Borlum, with two thousand men, to make contact with them, while he and the rest of his force stayed on in Perth. Old Borlum, as he was known, had seen some service in the French Army, and now, on his own initiative, made a quick dash for Edinburgh. He was, however, headed off by the no less experienced Argyll, and so continued southwards, joining Kenmure and Forster at Kelso. Thence their combined force struck south across the Border to Preston in Lancashire, where, thanks to the stupidity and inaction of the English Jacobites, they were soon forced to capitulate.

Mar, meanwhile, was still in Perth. When Argyll had left Stirling unprotected in order to save Edinburgh from Borlum he had, it is true, advanced as far as Dunblane, but only to fall back once more on Perth when Argyll returned. In the north, meanwhile, Lord Lovat, Chief of Clan Fraser, returning from France, where he had been in touch with King James, had raised his clan and seized Inverness Castle on behalf of King George, thereby regaining to

Highland dirks, swords and targe of the 17th and 18th centuries.

some extent the confidence of the English Court and Government, who up to then had, like everyone else, regarded him with suspicion. Such Frasers as had joined Mar accordingly now deserted, as did many of the Gordons, who were in due course followed by their Chief's son, Huntly. The Jacobite situation in the north was fast deteriorating. Soon the Whig clans, Sutherlands, Frasers, Mackays, Rosses and Munroes, were in more or less complete control there.

The news was now received that strong reinforcements of Government troops from Holland were on their way to join Argyll and, in the second week of November, Mar and his main force once more slowly advanced in the direction of Stirling. Argyll moved to meet him and on the morning of 13 November the two armies met at Sheriffmuir, a mile or two to the north of Dunblane.

At the outset of the engagement that followed, the Macleans and Macdonalds, on the right of the Jacobite line, threw off their plaids and charged the enemy with the claymore. For them something else was at stake besides just the future of this dynasty or the other. They were fighting once again for their existence as clans against their hereditary enemies, the all-pervading Campbells. 'Gentlemen,' said Maclean of Duart, a veteran of Killiecrankie, placing himself at the head of his Clan and looking across to where Argyll had drawn up his troops over against them, 'this is a day we have long wished to see. Yonder stands MacChailein Mor for King George. Here stands Maclean for King James. God bless Maclean and King James. Gentlemen, charge.' In the ensuing encounter the enemy's infantry were routed. But such was the enthusiasm of the clansmen on the right that they hardly noticed that their own centre and left had in the meanwhile been broken by Argyll's cavalry and driven back to Allan Water. In the event, neither side saw fit to risk a second round. Argyll now fell back on Dunblane, while Mar once again withdrew to Perth.

Militarily the battle had been indecisive. But in a wider sense it had been a defeat for the Jacobites. Argyll still held Stirling, thus blocking the way to England, whence the news soon arrived of the Jacobite surrender at Preston. The longer Mar sat at Perth, the worse his position became. His Highlanders, with nothing to do and little hope of plunder, faded back into the hills in ever larger numbers. Meanwhile Argyll's army had been joined by reinforcements from Holland as well as by the troops released by the Jacobite surrender at Preston. From being themselves heavily outnumbered, the Government forces now outnumbered their opponents by nearly three to one. Only heavy snow stopped them from at once attacking in strength.

Two-handed claymore, possibly 16th century, of the type used as late as the Rising of 1715.

Landing of Prince James Edward
at Peterhead in January 1716.

Such was the situation when on 22 December 1715 James Edward landed
at Peterhead. But 'Old Mr Melancholy' was not the man to restore a situation
that was already as good as lost. He himself was suffering from fever and ague,
while some gold sent him by the Spaniards had been lost at sea off Dundee.
'For me', he told his officers with gloomy resignation, 'it is no new thing to be
unfortunate, since my whole life from my cradle has been a constant series of
misfortunes.' It was not a speech to raise the spirits of already disheartened men.
Nor did his cold, reserved manner endear him to those he met.

At the end of January 1716 came the news that Argyll was advancing to the
attack, and to their utter dismay Mar's Highlanders now learned that it was their
leaders' intention to abandon Perth and retreat northwards. Worse still, on

The execution of the
Earl of Derwentwater
and Viscount Kenmure
on Tower Hill in 1716.
Along with many other
Jacobite leaders, their
titles and estates were
forfeited for their
adherence to Prince
James's cause.

The end of 'the Fifteen'. A contemporary engraving shows captured rebels on their way to London, and vignettes of episodes from the Rebellion.

reaching Montrose, James Edward and Mar, slipping away, secretly took ship to France. When the remaining Highlanders reached Aberdeen, a message was read out to them from James advising them to shift for themselves.

Having had this warning, the London Government now took what they considered the necessary measures to prevent another rising. Hundreds of Jacobites were sent to the plantations, two of the leaders who had failed to escape abroad were executed, and nineteen peerages and a number of estates were forfeited. An attempt was also made to disarm the clans, but this was only partly successful. Those clans whose loyalty was to London duly handed over their weapons, while the others turned in any obsolete weapons they no longer

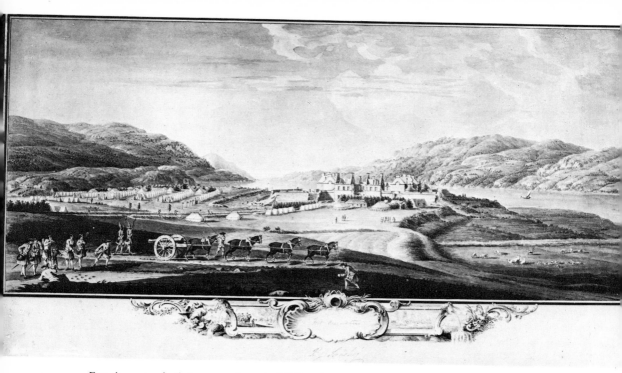

Fort Augustus, built in 1716 to keep the Highlanders in check. At that time called Kilchumin, it was enlarged by General Wade in 1730; after 'the Forty-Five' it was renamed in honour of the Duke of Cumberland.

needed and hid the rest for future use. The Union was now more unpopular than ever and even those Scots who supported the Hanoverians had come to resent the Government's attitude to their country.

The Jacobites, meanwhile, had found a new ally in Cardinal Alberoni, the all-powerful Minister of the King of Spain, and in 1719 it was agreed that Seaforth and the Earl Marischal, with two frigates and three hundred Spanish soldiers, should land on the west coast of Scotland to raise the clans, while a force of twenty-seven ships and five thousand soldiers sailed for England. But once again the Jacobites were dogged by ill fortune. A storm scattered the larger expedition before they could land. The party destined for Scotland duly landed on the shores of Loch Alsh and marched as far as Glenshiel. But here they found themselves confronted both by sea and by land with greatly superior Government forces. The Spaniards surrendered, while the Earl Marischal and the Scottish Jacobites who had joined him took to the hills and dispersed. On the other hand, some six thousand muskets that were landed seem in due course to have found their way into the hands for which they were intended.

The Government, for their part, persisted with their measures for the pacification and subjection of the Highlands. The native Gaelic or 'Irish' tongue, as they called it, had in particular long been a target for English and (more especially) Lowland Scottish reformers. Already in 1695 an Act had provided for the 'erecting of English Schools for rooting out of the Irish language and other pious uses' and in 1720 we are told that the design of the Society for the Propagation of Christian Knowledge was 'not to continue the Irish language, but to wear it out, and learn the people the English tongue'. A new and more stringent disarming Act was passed in 1725 and many Highlanders actually abandoned, for the time being, their habit of always carrying arms in public.

Meanwhile, General Wade, who had been appointed Commander-in-Chief for Scotland, embarked on a ten-year programme of military road-building, designed to penetrate the more important regions of the Highlands and link the strategic strongpoints of Fort William, Fort Augustus and Fort George. These roads which, when completed, covered 260 miles, gave the central Government a far greater measure of control over the Highlands than ever before and, by opening them up, did as much as anything to destroy the old order which still prevailed there. At the same time, a number of Independent Highland Companies, recruited from Whig clansmen and later formed into a regular regiment known as the Black Watch, were raised by General Wade, in the first place for police duties. The command of one of these companies was entrusted for a time to Lord Lovat, but later, much to his disgust, withdrawn.

General Wade's bridge, Aberfeldy, built in 1733 as part of a programme for improving communications in the Highlands.

In 1727 George II had succeeded George I. But there had been no change in the Government's attitude to Scotland and relations between Scotland and England showed no signs of improvement. Up to 1725 Scottish affairs had been handled in Whitehall by a separate Secretary for Scotland. Now, under the long premiership of Sir Robert Walpole, they passed into the province of the Home Secretary, while for most purposes executive power resided with Argyll or Forbes of Culloden, the Lord Advocate and later Lord President. Friction, of one kind or another, was constant. Resentment at taxes on malt and taxes on salt led to various outbursts of rioting in the cities. Smuggling became a patriotic duty, the excise-men public enemies and smugglers popular heroes. Finally in 1736 there was a major scandal, when a certain Captain Porteous, who had been sentenced to death by a Scottish court for firing on an angry crowd protesting at the public execution of a well-known smuggler, but subsequently reprieved, was taken from prison and hanged by 'persons unknown', acting, we are told, 'with the greatest secrecy, policy and vigour'.

To this rough justice Queen Caroline, who was acting as Regent during her husband's absence in his native Hanover, and the Government in London reacted with a Bill of Pains and Penalties. This required the City Charter of Edinburgh to be destroyed, the City Guard disbanded, the Netherbar Port demolished and the Provost imprisoned. And it was only thanks to the intervention of Argyll with Queen Caroline, who in her German way had taken what had happened as a personal insult and announced her intention of

The lynching of Captain Porteous in 1736. This painting by James Drummond, done in 1855, shows a large mob looking on; a contemporary account says that he was hanged 'with the greatest secrecy'.

Prince Charles Edward: portrait by Antonio David, 1732.

'making Scotland a hunting ground', that these outrageous penalties were not in fact enforced, a heavy fine being exacted from the City in their place.

None of this did anything to endear the House of Hanover to their Scottish subjects. And now tensions were building up in Europe which were to involve Britain in war, first with Spain in 1739 and then the following year with France. By 1742 a British army, the newly raised Black Watch with it, was fighting in the Netherlands and once again there was reasonable hope that a Jacobite rising might enjoy the active support of powerful allies.

The Jacobites had another asset. In James's elder son, Prince Charles Edward, they had at last a potential leader, a young man of energy, courage and personal magnetism, more than ready, if the chance offered, to fight for his rights and those of his house. In January 1744 Prince Charles took leave of his father in Rome and set out for France.

Prince Charles Edward

The French were at this moment planning to invade England with a sizeable fleet and an army of ten thousand men assembled at Dunkirk under the famous Marshal Saxe. In March the invasion fleet was dispersed by storms and the whole project had to be abandoned. In May of the following year, however, the French soundly defeated the English and Dutch at Fontenoy and Charles's

On the shore of Loch nan Uamh, in Moidart, Prince Charles takes leave of Antoine Walsh, who had conveyed him across the Minch from Eriskay. Contemporary drawing, given to Walsh by the Prince after his return to France.

hopes rose again. 'May I not trust', he wrote to Louis XV of France, 'that this signal victory which Your Majesty has just won over your enemies and mine (for they are one and the same) has resulted in some change in affairs; and that I may derive some advantage from this new blaze of glory which surrounds you?'

But this did not evoke from Louis the ready response that Charles had hoped for. Nor did the Scottish or English Jacobites show any great readiness to rise of their own accord. To Charles it now became evident that the best hope lay in bold action on his own part. Only thus could the reluctant Jacobites be persuaded to rise and the doubting French be convinced that his cause was worthy of support. And so, with money raised by pawning his mother's rubies, he fitted out a frigate, the *Dutellir* or *Doutelle* and a ship of the line, the *Elizabeth*, and with these set sail in July from Nantes for Scotland. After a sharp encounter with an English warship off the Lizard the *Elizabeth* was forced to put back into port, but the *Doutelle* escaped her pursuers and on 2 August 1745 Prince Charles, with seven supporters, landed on the Island of Eriskay in the Outer Hebrides.

The reception that greeted him was not encouraging. Macleod and Macdonald of Sleat, for all their past professions of loyalty, refused to have anything to do with him, while Macdonald of Boisdale anxiously urged him to go home. 'I am come home,' the Prince replied tersely and set sail with his seven companions for Moidart, where Macdonald of Clanranald at once rallied to his colours.

The news of his landing filled the mainland Jacobites with concern. Cameron of Lochiel, always a fervent supporter of the Stuarts, begged him in his turn to abandon the enterprise. But without success. 'Be the issue what it will,' Charles replied, 'I am determined to display my Standard and take the field with such as may join it. Lochiel, whom my father esteemed the best friend of our family, may stay at home, and learn his Prince's fate from the newspapers.' To this there could be only one answer. 'I'll share the fate of my Prince,' said Lochiel, 'and so shall every man over whom nature or fortune hath given me any power.' And so on 19 August, in Glenfinnan, before some nine hundred assembled Camerons and Macdonalds, the Standard was raised and James VIII and III once more proclaimed King.

From Glenfinnan the Prince boldly set out for Edinburgh, gathering support as he went. Soon nearly three thousand clansmen from the west had joined him, Camerons, Macleans and Macdonalds. On receiving news of what was happening, Sir John Cope, the English Commander-in-Chief, avoiding an engagement with the Prince's force in the Pass of Corryarrick, withdrew northwards towards Inverness, leaving open the way to the capital.

Having captured Perth, the Highlanders marched on Edinburgh. It was now mid-September. At Coltbridge they met two regiments of Government dragoons and routed them. In the city itself there was panic. The City Guard and Volunteers melted away, and when the Netherbar Port was opened to let a coach pass through, a party of Camerons rushed the sentries and gained control of the sleeping city. Next day King James VIII was proclaimed at the Market Cross and Charles entered Holyrood in triumph, 'met' we are told, 'by vast multitudes of people who by their repeated shouts and huzzas express'd a great deal of joy to see the Prince'. Only a few took a less enthusiastic view, speaking of 'a Popish Italian Prince, with the oddest crew that Britain could produce, with plaids, bagpipes, and bare buttocks . . . tag, rag and bobtail'.

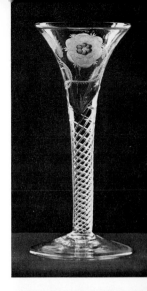

Toasting glasses, 18th century, for drinking to 'the King over the water'.

171

Entry of Prince Charles into Edinburgh, where his father was proclaimed King James VIII.

Prestonpans

General Cope, meanwhile, was at Aberdeen. The Frasers and the great Whig clans of the north had not, as he had hoped, rushed to his support; they were waiting to see what happened. Not wishing to be cut off completely, Cope rather shamefacedly piled his soldiers into some ships and, landing them at Dunbar, marched on Edinburgh. At Prestonpans he encountered the Prince who had come out to meet him. As often before, the regular infantry could not withstand the violence of the Highland charge. The thin red line wavered and broke; the Government artillery missed their opportunity; and Cope's two regiments of dragoons once again sought safety in flight. 'They ran', Charles wrote to his father, 'like rabets.' Meanwhile, leaving his troops to surrender to the insurgents, John Cope galloped into Berwick ahead of the advance party with the news of what had happened. 'The first general in Europe', it was afterwards said of him, 'who had brought the first tidings of his own defeat.'

His victory at Prestonpans gave Charles a high opinion of the troops under his command and of their potentialities. It also brought him fresh reinforcements. But he failed to follow up his advantage and lingered on in Edinburgh for more than a month, while George II's Government, now seriously disturbed, brought back more and more Dutch and English regular troops from Flanders and sent them to join old General Wade, now a Field-Marshal, at Newcastle. In London, meanwhile, a new verse had been added to the recently composed National Anthem and was sung nightly at Drury Lane to loud applause:

> *God grant that Marshal Wade*
> *May by thy mighty aid*
> > *Victory bring.*
> *May he sedition hush*
> *And like a torrent rush*
> *Rebellious Scots to crush.*
> > *God Save the King.*

Charles had hoped for active French support. Supplies came from France, and money, but no men. Further delay was impossible. In a letter to his father written from Edinburgh in October Charles put his own strength at eight thousand, and three hundred horse. 'With these, as matters stand,' he wrote, 'I shall have one decisive stroke for't. . . . I must either conquer or perish in a little while.' Again his best hope lay in boldness. At the beginning of November he crossed the border and started his advance on London.

'A Race from Preston Pans to Berwick': contemporary satirical comment on Sir John Cope's bringing the news of his own defeat.

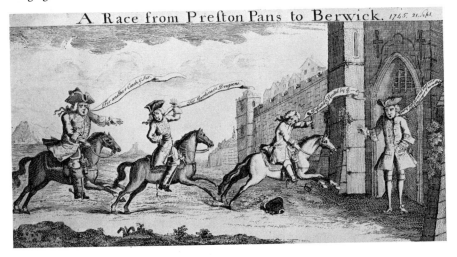

173

Lord George Murray, Prince Charles's Lieutenant-General. Portrait by an unknown artist.

Opposite: English foot guards saying farewell at the Tottenham Court Road turnpike before marching to Finchley to meet Prince Charles's forces. Engraving by William Hogarth.

Charles would have liked to begin by attacking Wade in Northumberland, but, on the pressing advice of Lord George Murray, his Lieutenant-General, he finally agreed to advance instead by way of Carlisle into Lancashire, where it was hoped that he would be joined by large numbers of English Jacobites. In the event this hope did not materialize. Though he met with no resistance to speak of in England, where the inhabitants were relieved to find that the Highlanders were not cannibals, as they had been led to expect, he was joined by only two or three hundred English recruits, mostly from Manchester, while already some of his Scottish troops, feeling homesick, were beginning to desert.

Wade, meanwhile, was threatening Prince Charles from the north-east with one army; George II's fat young son, the Duke of Cumberland, was advancing through the Midlands to meet him with another; while a third, of doubtful quality, was drawn up at Finchley for the defence of the English capital   in all some thirty thousand regular troops against no more than five thousand badly equipped Highlanders and a couple of hundred men from Manchester.

By the beginning of December the Highland army had reached Derby and there Charles held a council of war to decide on his next move. He was now only 130 miles from London. He had not suffered a single set-back. In the English capital there was panic. The Bank of England was paying in sixpences and George II was getting ready to go back to Hanover. It was a moment when

boldness offered the best, if not the only, hope of success. Counsels of prudence could only be counsels of despair. Charles, realizing this, wanted to continue his advance. 'I can see nothing', he said, 'but ruin and destruction to us in case we should retreat.'

But his advisers, led by Lord George Murray, only saw the obvious dangers of advancing further and in the end it was they who won the day. The decision was now taken to withdraw to the Highlands, where a new campaign, said Lord George, could be launched in the spring. At this Charles, in Lord Elcho's words, 'fell into a passion and gave most of the Gentlemen that spoke very Abusive Language and said that they had a mind to betray him.' For all this, on 6 December 1745 his army began their long march north and soon Horace Walpole in London was able to say that he was no longer afraid of 'a rebellion that runs away'.

On 19 December the Highlanders reached Carlisle and the following day crossed the Esk and were back once more on Scottish soil. But not necessarily, they found, on friendly territory. Dumfries was openly hostile and Glasgow not much better. In the Highlands, it was true, more clans had come out for the Prince, so that his numbers were again on the increase. But Seaforth (more accurately, Lord Fortrose) and his Mackenzies had joined the Hanoverian clans of the north, Sutherlands, Macleods, Mackays and Munroes. Lord Lovat, on the other hand, his interest aroused by the prospect of a Jacobite Dukedom,

The Duke of Cumberland receiving the surrender of Carlisle from the French commanding officer, 30th December 1745.

was now veering to Prince Charles, despite the urging of his old Whig friend Forbes of Culloden to do nothing of the kind.

In January 1746 Charles, continuing his march north, advanced on Stirling with seven or eight thousand men. At Falkirk he met the English General Hawley with a rather larger force of Government troops. Again the shock tactics of the Highlanders put the regulars to flight. But the battle was not decisive and again Charles did not follow up his advantage. Instead, he raised the siege of Stirling and, moving further north beyond the Tay, established his headquarters at Inverness. Once more frustration and inactivity took their toll; morale sagged and numbers dwindled.

All this time the Government had been bringing back more and more troops from Flanders. These were sent to Scotland and assembled at Aberdeen under the Duke of Cumberland, who spent six weeks there in careful preparation. In April 1746 Charles learned that Cumberland, with a well-armed, well-trained and above all, well-fed army, twice the size of his own, was advancing on Inverness.

On receiving this news, Charles made an effort to rally his troops and in the end gathered some five thousand hungry, ill-equipped Highlanders on Culloden

Moor outside Inverness. The site was essentially unfavourable to the semi-guerrilla tactics of the Highlanders, though well suited to regular troops. On 14 April Cumberland's army, having crossed the Spey, pitched their camp twelve miles away, outside the town of Nairn.

On the night of 15 to 16 April, Lord George Murray, who quite rightly 'did not like the ground' and hoped that surprise might help to redress the balance between the two armies, proposed a night attack on Cumberland's camp. But the plan miscarried. The Highlanders, who had only eaten one biscuit apiece the day before, spent half the night wandering about in the dark without ever finding the enemy. By the time they had made their way to their camp, they were completely worn out and slept where they dropped. At daybreak Cumberland gave his well-fed, well-trained and well-rested regulars the order to attack and the starving and exhausted Highlanders were dragged from their sleep by the sound of the enemy's drums beating to arms.

Cumberland began his attack with a heavy artillery barrage to which the Highlanders could make no effective reply. After this had lasted for an hour, and more and more gaps began to show in their ranks, they began to grow restive and the Prince told Lord George Murray to give the order to charge. The

The Battle of Culloden, 16th April 1746. An anonymous engraving, published a few weeks after the battle, shows the scene in front of Culloden House as the Young Chevalier, on horseback, flees before the Duke of Cumberland.

Macdonalds, who traditionally claimed the right of the line, had been placed on the left and were therefore disgruntled. In the centre the Camerons, Clan Chattan, the Macleans and the Maclachlans came first to the shock. 'They came running upon our front line like troops of hungry wolves,' a soldier of the Royal Scots from Ayr wrote to his wife next day. But this time the Hanoverians were ready for the Highland charge. 'Nothing', says Colonel Whitefoord of the Fifth Marines, 'could be more desperate than their attack or more properly received.' Having broken through Cumberland's first line and engaged the second, the Highlanders found themselves caught between two fires and died by hundreds on the Hanoverian bayonets.

With the regular English and Lowland Scottish Regiments stood four companies of Argyll's men – his 'brave Campbells', as Cumberland called them. And now the enemy cavalry were charging down on the Jacobites. '*Allein*', said old Maclean of Drimnin, on learning from his son Allan that his other son Lachlan was dead, '*comma leat misse, mas toil leat do bheatha thoir'n arrigh dhuit fhein*' – 'Do not think of me, take care of yourself if you value your life.' Then, with his wig and bonnet gone, the old man, who had once served in the Royal Navy, turned to face the enemy. 'It shall not be for naught,' he said, and, cutting down the first English dragoon who came at him, managed to wound another before three more rode up out of the smoke and finished him off.

This old cottage, on the battlefield, is the only building to survive the Battle of Culloden.

Captain Grosett of the King's troops, shot by one of Prince Charles's men whom he had captured.

On the left, meanwhile, the Macdonalds, outflanked by the English cavalry, had been mown down by grapeshot before they could come to grips with the enemy. Already all over the field the English troopers were riding down and butchering the Highland wounded.

Prince Charles, it is said, watched the rout of his army with tears in his eyes. When it was complete, he let himself be led from the field by one of his officers. 'There you go for a damned cowardly Italian,' was the blunt Lowland comment of Lord Elcho, who himself lived to publish a valuable account of his experiences during the Rising.

179

Flora Macdonald, after a portrait by Allan Ramsay.

For the next five months Prince Charles, with a price of £30,000 on his head, wandered, a hunted fugitive with sometimes only two or three companions, through the western Highlands and Islands. The £30,000, he was assured by the poor Highlanders he encountered, could be no temptation to them, because anyone who earned it would be ashamed ever to show himself in the Highlands again. And so, thanks to the loyalty and resourcefulness of his friends and possibly to the half-heartedness of some of those who were supposed to be searching for him, he was never captured by the Government troops with whom the whole area was now swarming. From South Uist, where he first took refuge, he made his way across to Skye and thence back to the mainland. Through all the hazards and hardships of those strenuous months, Charles showed unfailing courage and cheerfulness and won the hearts and devotion of all he met. It was in a sense his fulfilment, something that had never been vouchsafed him before and never would be again. At last on 19 September 1746 he was, with difficulty, picked up by a French frigate from the shores of the same sea-loch where he had landed fourteen months before, and thence carried safely back to France, to spend the rest of his life as an unhappy exile. *Bliadna Thearlaich*, Charlie's Year, as the Highlanders called it, was over.

'The Agreable Contrast' between Prince Charles with Flora Macdonald, and Butcher Cumberland with a town trollop. For once, pictorial propaganda for the losing side.

Chapter Seven

'FOR A' THAT'

The Rising of 1745 gave the Government in London a nasty fright. 'I tremble with fear,' wrote Cumberland, 'that this vile spot may still be the ruin of this island and our family.' It also offered them and their friends in Scotland the opportunity they had long been seeking for a final reckoning with the High, landers. In Cumberland they found the ideal instrument for this task. He carried it out with characteristically Teutonic thoroughness and gusto.

After Culloden no quarter was given. Hundreds of Jacobite wounded were, on the Duke's express instructions, shot as they lay on the field of battle. Some, where it was more convenient, were burned alive. Such prisoners as were taken were treated in such a way that they died by hundreds. Meanwhile detachments of Government troops, both Scottish and English, were sent out into the territory of the clans who had been loyal to Prince Charles to hunt down the fugitives, loot and burn the houses, drive away the cattle and devastate the country. When the Provost of Inverness, a good Whig, came to plead for better treatment for his countrymen, he was kicked downstairs. And when Forbes of Culloden, who in his way had done more than anyone to further the Hanoverian cause in the Highlands, appealed for less brutality, he was dismissed by Cumberland as 'that old woman who spoke to me of humanity'. In May 1746, to crown his triumph, the Duke received an official address from the General Assembly of the Church of Scotland which praised his conduct and valour in the most effusive terms and even spoke of the 'public blessings' conferred by his family 'on mankind'.

The Government followed up Cumberland's victory with a series of acts of policy designed to prevent any risk of a Jacobite revival by crushing the spirit of the Highlanders and destroying the Highland way of life. The Episcopal

William Augustus, Duke of Cumberland. Portrait by Sir Joshua Reynolds.

Church, which was suspected of favouring the Jacobite cause, was more deliberately and methodically persecuted than ever. Most of the Jacobite leaders who had not died in battle or escaped abroad were tried and executed and hundreds of clansmen were sent to the plantations. Even the aged Lovat, who with less than his usual flexibility had brought his Clan in at the last moment on the losing side, was taken to the Tower of London and, like his ancestor four centuries before, beheaded, a fate which he met with commendable dignity and courage. As he was being taken to the place of execution, the throng of spec/tators was so great that one of the stands collapsed and a number of people were killed. 'The more the mischief', was the old man's characteristic comment, 'the better the sport.'

Disarming the Clans

Meanwhile the lands of the Jacobite chiefs were forfeited and a determined attempt was made to destroy the clan system once and for all. A special Disarming Act was evolved by Lord Hardwicke, the Lord Chancellor, whose son Joseph had been present at Culloden as Cumberland's *aide-de-camp*. This Act, which was passed in 1746, imposed severe penalties not only for carrying or possessing arms, but for wearing the kilt, plaid or any other tartan garment. Even the pipes were prohibited as 'an instrument of war'. At the same time, the heritable jurisdictions of the chiefs were abolished and various other measures taken to break their power and destroy their old patriarchal relationship with their clan. The Government's policy led in the long run to large-scale emigration and drew from Dr Samuel Johnson, who was certainly not unduly prejudiced in Scotland's

Simon, Lord Lovat, on trial for treason. He was found guilty, taken to the Tower, and beheaded.

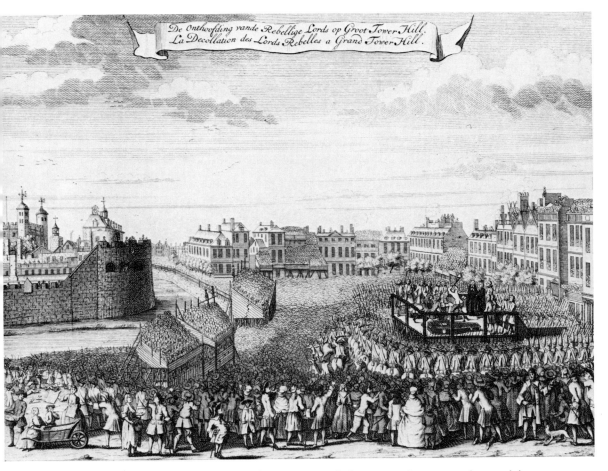

De Onthoofding vande Rebellige Lords op Groot Tower Hill.
La Decollation des Lords Rebelles a Grand Tower Hill.

Execution of two rebel Lords on Tower Hill, before a great crowd of spectators. So great was the crowd that one of the stands collapsed, killing several people.

favour, the acid comment that 'to govern peaceably by having no subjects is an expedient that argues no great profundity of policy'. His words recalled, per-haps consciously, the speech which seventeen centuries before Tacitus had put into the mouth of the Caledonian hero Calgacus, '*solitudinem faciunt, pacem appellant*'.

But for all this, something of the old spirit lingered on. Spies sent out by Lord Albemarle, now Commander-in-Chief in Scotland, reported that the Macleans, Grants of Glenmoriston, Macphersons, Macdonells of Glengarry and Camerons, were all eager 'to do it again', if only help could be obtained from France. On 15 May 1752 Campbell of Glenure, while engaged in evicting tenants from the forfeited Jacobite lands of Lochiel and of Ardshiel in Appin, was shot dead

183

in broad daylight by a marksman who, thanks to good planning and the wide-spread sympathy his action commanded, got clean away, though the Duke of Argyll and a Campbell jury saw to it that another, innocent man was hanged in his place. And even as late as 1770 secret agents were to report to Argyll that the Macleans were once more 'stirring'.

But by now there was no longer any real hope for the Jacobite cause. Prince Charles, since 1766, in his turn, 'King over the water' and now belatedly a Protestant, was living in a rented Italian palace with the Royal Arms of Great Britain painted in the entrance hall and on the roof a weathervane, which to this day still bears the Royal cypher CRIII, a pathetic, rather drunken elderly gentleman with a disagreeable, unfaithful German wife and no legitimate child. His only comfort besides the bottle was his natural daughter Charlotte, Burns's 'bonie Lass of Albany', on whom he bestowed much affection and the title of Duchess of Albany and who, though she never married, managed to bear three children to the Archbishop of Bordeaux. Sometimes, we are told, a visitor or a member of Charles's entourage would sing *Lochaber no more* or some other Jacobite song and tears would come to his bleary eyes at the memories it recalled.

Signature of Charles Edward on a letter to his banker, *c.* 1773. His father being dead, he signs 'Charles R.', King Charles III.

Opposite: marble tomb, in St Peter's, Rome, of James III, Charles Edward, and his brother Henry. It was paid for by King George III.

IACOBO·III
IACOBI·II·MAGNAE·BRIT·REGIS·FILIO
KAROLO·EDVARDO
ET·HENRICO·DECANO·PATRVM·CARDINALIVM
IACOBI·III·FILIIS
REGIAE·STIRPIS·STVARDIAE·POSTREMIS
ANNO·M·DCCC·XIX

BEATI·MORTVI
QVI·IN·DOMINO·MORIVNTVR

The General Assembly of the Kirk of Scotland 1787

General Assembly of the Church of Scotland, in Tron Church, Edinburgh, in 1787. The Earl of Dalhousie presides (right), and the orator at the bar (left) is James Boswell.

Opposite: George IV in his kilt: portrait by Sir David Wilkie.

Reconciliation

On Charles's death in 1788 he was succeeded as head of the House of Stuart by his younger brother Henry, Cardinal York, who by entering the Church had effectively destroyed the prospects of his dynasty, but nevertheless now assumed the style of Henry IX. In 1807 he, too, died. Twelve years later a fine marble tomb was erected to the two brothers and to their father in St Peter's by the generosity of their distant relative and legal successor, King George III of England, now mentally disturbed and almost on his own deathbed. In 1822 the latter's ebullient son, George IV, his plump limbs draped in what he had been told was the Royal Stuart tartan, paid a state visit to Scotland, the first

member of his own family to do so since his great-great-uncle William Duke of Cumberland nearly eighty years earlier and the first reigning monarch of any dynasty since Charles II's brief though eventful sojourn in 1650. He was greeted with enthusiasm by Sir Walter Scott, who for his part was wearing Campbell tartan and by many others, and was entertained in tremendous style by Lord Hopetoun, whose father in his day had taken the trouble to ride out in his coach to welcome the conquering Duke of Cumberland on his return from Culloden.

Queen Victoria stepping ashore from a boat at Loch Muich, in her 'dear Highlands'. This water-colour sketch for an oil-painting is by Sir Edwin Landseer (*c.* 1850).

But any previous neglect by its monarchs of the northern part of the United Kingdom was to be more than made up for by the assiduous attention it subsequently received from George IV's indomitable niece, Queen Victoria, who with her brightly kilted consort, Prince Albert of Saxe-Coburg-Gotha, regularly spent her summer holidays there, describing them day by day and in great detail in her *Journal of Our Life in the Highlands*. 'We were always', she wrote in an explanatory footnote, 'in the habit of conversing with the Highlanders – with whom one comes so much in contact in the Highlands. The Prince highly appreciated the good-breeding, simplicity, and intelligence which make it so pleasant and even instructive to talk to them.' And again: 'The view was so beautiful over the dear hills; the day so fine; the whole *so gemüthlich.*'

Edinburgh Castle, by Paul Sandby
(*c. 1750*).

It was a tradition that was to be happily continued by Victoria's successors. In the years that followed, the Crown, most appropriately, was to serve as the strongest link between Scotland and the rest of the United Kingdom, while by his marriage to the daughter of an ancient Scottish family King George VI was to bring to his dynasty a stronger native strain than it had enjoyed since James VI and I had rumbled south in his state coach with his bag of golf clubs slung behind. Again, in the present reign the Queen, by more than once attending the General Assembly of the Church of Scotland and by taking up residence each year at Holyroodhouse, has stirred the imagination and roused the enthusiasm of her Scottish subjects, who thus see Edinburgh once more playing its proper role as capital of their country.

In 1707 the most attractive thing to Scotland about the Union with England had been the economic advantages she hoped to derive from it. But it was some considerable time before these began to be felt. Indeed the immediate effect of the Union was to make things worse for Scotland than they were already. By the middle of the eighteenth century, however, a flourishing trade had been built up in tobacco shipped from the American colonies for re-export to the Continent. Big fortunes were made by the swaggering red-cloaked 'tobacco lords' and Glasgow was soon the biggest tobacco port in Great Britain. At the same time a flourishing new linen industry grew up and linen became Scotland's most important export.

Advantages of the Union

With the American War of Independence, however, the situation changed. The Americans were now free to sell their own tobacco anywhere in the world and the profitable tobacco trade collapsed. Much of the available capital thus released was to go into building up the new cotton industry, which in its turn superseded linen and dominated the Scottish economy for the next hundred years.

By the end of the eighteenth century the simple, mainly rural economy of Scotland had been replaced by a more complex one. People no longer necessarily lived from the produce of their own districts. In the Clyde Valley and elsewhere, industrial areas, accompanied by corresponding concentrations of population, were beginning to grow up.

For another sixty years cotton remained dominant. Then, in the 1860's, the American Civil War cut off supplies of raw cotton and the cotton industry collapsed as suddenly as the tobacco trade had done ninety years before. From textiles, the emphasis now shifted to heavy industry, and stayed there. As the nineteenth century went on, iron, steel, coal, engineering and shipbuilding in particular played an ever more dominant part. Before long Clydeside was

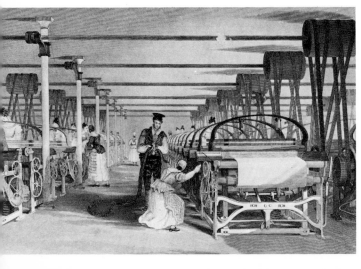

Power-loom weaving – an early form of industrialization.

Weighing the bar-lead, by David Allan (c. 1790).

leading the world in shipbuilding. Great fortunes were made and soon the ornate residences of the new rich lined the Firth of Clyde. But, as later generations were to discover to their cost, the basis of the economy was now dangerously narrow and had lost much of its earlier flexibility.

At the time of the Union Scotland, and the Highlands in particular, had possessed comparatively few roads. With increasing economic development, better means of transport became a necessity. And soon a regular system of roads covered the country. In the Highlands General Wade's strategic roads, built originally for military purposes, served as the starting-point for a more comprehensive road system. At the same time bridges were built and canals dug, the Forth and Clyde and the Caledonian being the most important. Scottish inventors and Scottish engineers led the world and in the 1840's, following the invention of the steam engine by James Watt of Greenock, Scotland was struck, like the rest of Great Britain, with railway mania and the road and canal

James Watt in his workshop. His invention of the separate condenser gave the steam-engine real power for the first time.

Opening of the Glasgow and Garnkirk Railway, 1831. View from St Collox, looking south-east.

The steam-paddle tug *Charlotte Dundas* and the paddle steamer *Comet*, two pioneering Scottish steamships.

systems were supplemented by a railway network which soon linked all the principal towns with each other and with the rest of the United Kingdom. In 1802 the *Charlotte Dundas* and in 1812 the *Comet* put Scotland as far ahead in steam navigation as in shipbuilding. Up to the time of the Union, the Scottish economy had been primarily agricultural, and despite growing industrialization, agriculture still remained of the utmost economic importance. Here, too, important changes were taking place. Old-fashioned methods of farming were discarded and new, more up-to-date methods introduced in their place.

Grinding corn by hand, and 'walking the cloth' – a primitive method of fulling cloth with the bare feet. From Pennant's *Tour in Scotland* (1774–6).

In the Highlands, the developments which followed the Union and the Risings of 1715 and 1745 were less happy. By the legislation with which they sought to break the clan system and by destroying the old patriarchal links between the chief and his clan, the London Government had succeeded in turning the surviving chiefs, whether Jacobite or Whig, into mere landed proprietors, some, though by no means all of whom no longer felt the same sense of responsibility for their clansmen and dependants as formerly, but, in difficult times, were more concerned with making their estates pay. The easiest method of doing this, most of them found, was to turn them over to sheep farming. For this large areas of land were required and so, in many parts of the Highlands, farms were cleared and taken over and tenants dispossessed and evicted, those responsible sometimes expediting matters by burning the houses of any who were slow to leave. Some of those thus thrown on the world turned, where they could, to crofting or fishing. Others emigrated to America or enlisted in the newly formed Highland regiments. Thousands more drifted into the already overcrowded cities and industrial areas. Beginning in the second half of the eighteenth century, the process, justified as often as not by reference to the most progressive Liberal principles, continued for the best part of a hundred years, culminating in the notorious Sutherland clearances which continued well into the reign of Queen Victoria. Soon in the glens little heaps of stones

Eviction of tenant-farmers went on all over the Highlands, from the 1760's onwards, as farms were cleared to make way for the easier profits of sheep.

Glasgow, a town of 12,000 at the time of the Union, had reached a million by the unlovely 1930's. View from the Necropolis.

amid the grass and nettles were all that remained of what once had been sizeable *clachans* and townships.

But while, after an initial increase, the population of the Highlands eventually dwindled, that of the cities and industrial areas increased by leaps and bounds. From 1,608,420 in 1801, the population of Scotland as a whole had grown by 1911 to 4,760,904. To the thousands of uprooted Highlanders were added in the 1840's vast numbers of starving Irish immigrants, driven from their homes by the potato famine and ready to accept any standard of living and any wage that would feed them. Low wages and long working hours were the rule. The expanding industries could absorb any amount of cheap labour. In the first forty years of the nineteenth century 350,000 people moved into the Clyde valley. From 12,000 at the time of the Union, the population of Glasgow rose to 77,000 in 1800 and to over 200,000 by 1830. By 1931 it had reached a million. That of the other industrial towns increased in like proportion. The result of this sudden growth was fearful overcrowding and appalling living conditions with disastrous consequences for the health and general well-being of the popula-

tion. Nor was any serious attempt made to improve things until well into the second half of the nineteenth century.

In the course of the hundred years that followed the Union, while Scotland was being completely transformed economically and socially, the political life of the country remained to all intents and purposes at a standstill. At times after 1707 the responsibility for Scottish affairs was officially entrusted to a Secretary for Scotland and at others to the British Secretary of State in charge of Home Affairs. But in practice power in Scotland resided with a political manager or boss, sometimes a private individual, who, owing to his personal influence and power of patronage, found himself able to manipulate the votes of the forty-five Scottish Members in the Westminster Parliament.

Of the latter, thirty represented the counties and the remaining fifteen the sixty-five royal burghs. The country franchise was still based on the medieval concept that Parliament was an assembly of the King's tenants, a system which made it possible to produce new voters at will by legally subdividing Crown tenancies without the lands involved ever changing hands. Even so the number of actual voters in Scotland remained small. With a total of 235 voters in 1781, Ayrshire possessed the largest electorate of any Scottish county. The Sheriffdom of Bute, on the other hand, could only boast 12. In 1788 the total for the whole country was under 3,000.

The system of franchise obtaining in the royal burghs bore even less relation to democracy. The burgh Members were not elected by the burgesses nor, save in the case of Edinburgh, directly by the town councils, but by delegates appointed for the purpose by groups of four or five burghs. The wholesale redistribution of population which followed the Industrial Revolution still further exaggerated the defects of the system. Large new centres of population, such as Paisley and Greenock, which were not royal burghs, had no representation at all, while three of the fifteen burgh Members were returned by the Fife Burghs, several of which had long ceased to be more than hamlets.

Such a system clearly lent itself to corruption and manipulation. The London Government had in its gift innumerable appointments, benefits and preferments, both at home and overseas, the promise of which, at a time when the ballot was not secret, was more than enough to swing this voter or that in the desired direction. 'Has a family to provide for', 'Sons in the army', 'His son wants a Kirk' are significant notes on a list of country voters for 1788. And the small total number of votes made the task of the party manager even easier.

During the earlier part of the eighteenth century Scotland was managed in the Whig interest by two successive Dukes of Argyll and later in that of the Tories by the most famous manager of all, Henry Dundas, first Viscount Melville, who in effect governed Scotland for thirty years. From Lord Advocate, Dundas, who became the close friend and political ally of William Pitt the younger, went on to be President of the Board of Control for India, Treasurer of the Navy, Home Secretary and Secretary for War, all of which offices in turn provided him with ample opportunities for patronage both at home and abroad and enabled him to keep the great majority of the forty-five Scottish Members and their constituents happy and loyal to the Tory cause. Only once, at the beginning of his career in 1778, when he sought to secure the passage of a Bill relieving Scottish Roman Catholics of some of the disabilities imposed on them, did he find that he had overreached himself and was obliged to bow before the storm of indignation which his proposal aroused.

Though less popular with those he passed over, Dundas achieved some useful reforms. His connection by marriage with a great west Highland family may have given him some understanding of Highland problems and he certainly

Henry Dundas

Henry Dundas, first Viscount Melville. A close friend of the younger Pitt, he 'managed' Scotland in the Tory interest for thirty years.

tried, however belatedly, to right some of the wrongs which the Hanoverians had inflicted on the Highlands. Thanks to him, Lord Hardwicke's preposterous Act of 1746, proscribing Highland dress and the playing of the pipes, was finally repealed in 1782, and in 1784 most of the forfeited Jacobite estates were returned to their rightful owners.

Already during the Seven Years War the elder Pitt had taken the controversial step of raising a number of Highland regiments, recruited from clansmen who barely a dozen years before had fought for Prince Charlie at Culloden. 'I sought', he said, 'for merit wherever it was to be found. It is my boast that I was the first Minister who looked for it and found it in the mountains of the north. I called it forth and drew into your service a hardy and intrepid race of men. . . . They served with fidelity as they fought with valour and conquered for you in every part of the world.' To Lord Hardwicke, on the other hand, he cynically commended his decision on other grounds, namely that 'not many of them would return'. Thus his policy served a double purpose. It provided King George II and his heirs with some of the finest soldiers in the world. And at the same time it denuded the Highlands of manpower and so removed a potential threat to the House of Hanover.

In 1805 Dundas, now First Lord of the Admiralty, was impeached for peculation. Although he was duly acquitted and restored to the Privy Council, his position was never again quite the same. On his death in 1811, however, he was succeeded by his son, who managed Scotland in his stead until his own death sixteen years later, when the task fell to a succession of less remarkable Lord Advocates.

In such circumstances it was perhaps not unnatural that the Scottish people should have sunk into a state of political apathy. 'When we had a King, and a Chancellor and Parliament men o' oor ain', says one of Sir Walter Scott's characters, 'we could aye peeble them wi' stanes when they werena guid bairns – but naebody's nails can reach the length o' Lunnon.' When a Scottish interest was directly attacked by some tax or other, there was an occasional display of resentment, which usually took the form of riots. Otherwise, the task of running the country was readily left to the manager of the day and his forty-five followers, who, for their part, were glad enough to do as they were told and accept the appropriate reward. Indeed one of the few recorded complaints from a Scottish Member was that the Lord Advocate of the day was not tall enough. 'The Scottish Members', he explained, 'always vote with the Lord Advocate, and we therefore require to see him in a division. Now, I can see Mr Pitt, and I can see Mr Addington, but I cannot see the Lord Advocate.'

The Giant Factotum amusing himself. Cartoon by James Gillray satirizing Pitt's dominance over the House of Commons. Dundas, in a kilt, supports his right foot, while his left crushes the Opposition. Even Mr Speaker doffs his cap to the 'Great Commoner'.

198

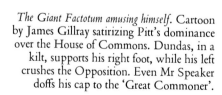

The GIANT-FACTOTUM amusing himself.

It was in this frame of mind that the fact of the Union, once so bitterly and so widely resented, came during the next hundred years or so to be generally accepted. But from this it was a long step to active Scottish participation in the political life of Westminster.

Only twice in the second half of the eighteenth century did informed Scottish opinion concern itself with questions of external policy. One occasion was the American War of Independence, when Scottish opinion, ignoring the generally subservient attitude of its parliamentary representatives, showed itself on the whole sympathetic to the colonists. The other was the outbreak of the French Revolution, when the new ideas found a ready response in Scotland. On both occasions, it was only natural that parallels should be drawn between the political rights of Scotsmen and those of Americans and Frenchmen. And the sympathy shown in Scotland for the ideas of the French Revolutionaries was strong enough to provoke savage reprisals from the authorities. Thus, Thomas Palmer, a minister of religion, was sent to Botany Bay for seven years and Thomas Muir, an advocate, sentenced to fourteen years' transportation, the judge in each case being the notorious Lord Braxfield. With the onset of the Napoleonic

Thomas Muir, an Edinburgh advocate. After a travesty of a trial before Lord Braxfield, he was sentenced to fourteen years' transportation to Botany Bay for the crime of urging reform of Parliament and extension of the franchise.

The Academy of Fine Arts, Glasgow. Its foundation in 1753 was part of a general flowering of the arts in Scotland.

David Hume.

Allan Ramsay: self-portrait, 1776.

Wars, however, and the rumoured threat of a French invasion, the Scots, many thousands of whom were now fighting for King George III in various British regiments and in the Royal Navy, began to feel increasing solidarity with their English neighbours.

Meanwhile, though Scottish politics were stagnant and Scotland was denied the means of political self-expression, the second half of the eighteenth century and the beginning of the nineteenth witnessed a great flowering of literature and of the arts and of the intellectual life of the country in general. Edinburgh, though now no longer the capital of an independent state, became one of the great literary, intellectual and artistic centres of Europe. This was the age of David Hume and Adam Smith, of Allan Ramsay and Raeburn, of David Wilkie and the Nasmyths, of Robert Adam and his brothers, of Macpherson's *Ossian* and the Celtic Revival, of Robert Burns and Walter Scott. Scotland might no longer be independent, but in men's minds her sense of nationhood was as strong as ever. 'Is it not strange', wrote David Hume in 1757, 'that, at a time when we have lost our Princes, our Parliaments, our independent Government, even the Presence of our chief Nobility, are unhappy in our Accent & Pronunciation, speak a very corrupt Dialect of the Tongue in which we make use of; is it not strange, I say, that, in these circumstances, we shou'd really be the People most distinguish'd for Literature in Europe?'

Opposite: Adam-style stair-well in Laurieston House, Glasgow.

Sir Walter Scott with his friends: he gave Scotland back her history.

But Robert Burns and Walter Scott did more than spread Scotland's fame abroad throughout the civilized world. They helped to restore to the Scots themselves the self-confidence and self-respect which the events of the past century had done so much to destroy, to dispel the unhappy feeling of inferiority and lost identity which had followed the Union. In particular both writers helped to create a new, popular image of Scotland and the Scots, which, though not always very closely related to reality, certainly served to put our country and nation back on the map. To such an extent that, from being regarded as uncouth barbarians inhabiting an insalubrious region north of the Tweed, the Scots soon became in the popular imagination paragons of all the virtues, at once fearless heroes and shrewd, merry, honest, hospitable folk with their hearts in the right place and their heads screwed on the right way, while Scotland

Robert Burns: he gave Scots a
new idea of themselves.

and the Highlands in particular became the goal of innumerable enthusiastic
sightseers from all over the world. Soon every Englishman was busy finding
himself a Scottish great-grandmother and the children of half Europe were
tricked out in fancy tartans *à la Lucia di Lammermoor*.

In Burns's poems, with their stress on tolerance and broadmindedness and
their strong emphasis on human nature with all its virtues and all its short-
comings, the Scots could see themselves with new pride as 'men for a' that', as
human beings more human than most, warm-hearted and open-handed to a
fault, great drinkers and lovers and sturdy fighters for freedom and the rights of
man. Sir Walter, for his part, gave Scotland back her history, a history of which
all could be proud and in which all could see themselves and their forebears in a
dramatic and romantic, if occasionally somewhat idealized light. Soon, with
the help of Macpherson's *Ossian*, the Ettrick Shepherd and a generation of neo-
Jacobite poetesses, was born, in place of the harsh, bloodstained reality, a happy
many-hued mythology of Celtic heroes, Robert the Bruce, Mary Queen of

Colonel Alastair Macdonell of
Glengarry, said to have been the
original of 'Fergus MacIvor' in
Waverley.

Scots, Rob Roy, Bonnie Prince Charlie and Flora Macdonald, which, at some slight cost to the cause of historical accuracy, has held the limelight ever since.

Meanwhile, the building of Britain's growing Empire offered the people of Scotland new scope for their special energies and talents. Sir Walter Scott had spoken of 'the national disposition to wandering and adventure', and the part played in this by the Scots was certainly out of all proportion to their numbers. 'A race of men', wrote James Barrie, 'the wind of whose name has swept the ultimate seas.' In every continent the lead was taken by Scottish explorers, soldiers, sailors, administrators, diplomats, merchants, engineers, missionaries, and doctors, who found abroad the opportunities that were denied them at home. This was the age of Mungo Park, of David Livingstone, of Colin Campbell, of Abercrombie and of innumerable others. And Scotland's part in this gave her in the long run a feeling of ever greater unity with the rest of Britain and of shared responsibility for the Empire she had helped to build.

Church Affairs
In Church matters, while the moderates in the Church of Scotland gradually came to accept their position as members of the Established Church, the Evangelicals found it less easy to reconcile themselves to the control of a Parliament the vast majority of whose members were neither Scottish nor Presbyterian. Trouble arose in particular over the question of patronage, which had been restored shortly after the Union and was not finally abolished until 1874. At the General Assembly of 1842 matters came to a head over Parliament's right to intervene in the affairs of the Church and in 1843 over four hundred ministers, more than a third of the total number, walked out of the Assembly and of the Established Church, followed by a like proportion of their parishioners, and, abandoning churches, manses and stipends, formed the Free Church of Scotland under their leader Thomas Chalmers. In 1900 the Free Church joined the so-called United Presbyterians to form the United Free Church, which could now muster 1,700 ministers as against 1,400 in the Church of Scotland. Finally in 1929, after the virtual abdication by the Westminster Parliament of its right to interfere in Church affairs in Scotland, a union was effected between the Church of Scotland and the United Free Church on terms satisfactory to both, thus uniting the great majority of Scottish Presbyterians in one Church.

The Episcopal Church, meanwhile, had been kept alive as a separate denomination by those members of the Church of Scotland who refused to accept the Settlement of 1690, and had, owing to the attachment of many of its adherents to the Jacobite cause, been vigorously persecuted throughout the eighteenth century. The penal laws against it were finally repealed in 1792, by when it had in Scott's words been reduced to 'the shadow of a shade'. But, though its numbers now increased, its membership was never to amount to more than a very small percentage of the total population.

As for the Roman Catholic Church, it had by the end of the seventeenth century virtually become extinct as an organized body in Scotland, its numbers dwindling to a few thousands, who lived for the most part in the remoter western Highlands and Islands, to which the influence of the Reformation had as yet scarcely penetrated. Partly as a result of missions from the continent of Europe there was some increase during the eighteenth century and by 1800 the total had reached about thirty thousand. During the nineteenth century, however, the number of Roman Catholics was enormously increased by large-scale Irish immigration, until in the Glasgow area it amounted to nearly one-third of the population – a third who distinguished themselves from the city's native Scottish inhabitants in a number of other ways besides religion. These differences and divergences were in due course to find ready expression on and around the football field, where the massively attended contests of Celtic and Rangers have become an increasingly important feature of our national life.

With the passing into law of the Scottish Reform Bill of 1832, which followed the stormy passage of the English Act of 1832, Scottish politics acquired a new vitality. Thanks to the creation of eight new burghs, the number of Scottish Members in the House of Commons was increased from forty-five to fifty-three. Edinburgh and Glasgow were now given two Members each and some of the new centres of population were at long last represented in Parliament. At the last election before the Reform, just thirty-nine electors had voted in Edinburgh. At the first election that followed it the number of voters under the extended franchise was over nine thousand.

Following the reform of Parliament and the reorganization of local government which accompanied it, the people of Scotland began to take more interest in politics. The old system of management by political bosses came to an end, and there was a wholesale change in the political complexion of the Members of Parliament that Scotland sent to Westminster. Under the Dundas regime all but six out of forty-five had been Tories. In the reformed Parliament forty-four out of fifty-three were Liberals. This Liberal ascendancy in Scotland was to last for the best part of a century. At only one general election between 1832 and 1917 did Scotland fail to return a majority of Liberal Members to

Scots at Westminster

Parliament. And as lately as 1922 twenty-eight out of the seventy-four Scottish Members were still Liberals. After this the fortunes of the Liberal Party in Scotland declined rapidly, until by the middle of the present century there was only one Scottish Liberal Member of Parliament. Nor has the promise of a second Liberal revival as yet been fulfilled.

The Reform Act of 1832 had enfranchised the middle class. Those of 1868 and 1885 further widened the franchise, while also increasing the number of Scottish Members to sixty and seventy-two respectively. In 1918 this was brought up to seventy-four and universal male adult suffrage introduced.

By the end of the eighteenth century, the Scottish cotton weavers had formed a trade union and during the first half of the nineteenth century strikes were organized in a number of industries in protest against the atrocious working conditions then prevailing. It was not, however, until the second half of the century that the trade-union movement took shape. In 1886 the Scottish Miners' Federation was formed with James Keir Hardie as its secretary and by 1892 there were 150,000 trade-union members in Scotland.

Side by side with the trade-union movement came the rise of the Scottish Labour Party. This was founded as an autonomous political body in 1888 by Keir Hardie and by R. B. Cunninghame Graham, a romantically minded writer and landowner. Its programme included, at that time, the nationalization of land, the abolition of the House of Lords, the disestablishment of the

James Keir Hardie, founder with Cunninghame Graham of the Scottish Labour Party in 1888.

206

Church and Home Rule for Scotland. It was later merged in the British Labour Party, but, although it lost its separate identity, the Scottish section of the Party was to act as a vitalizing influence to the Party as a whole during the 1920's and 1930's. In 1922, despite a decisive Conservative victory in England, Labour won thirty out of the seventy-four Scottish seats. Henceforth, with the decay of the Liberal Party, political power in Scotland was, over the years, to be more or less evenly balanced between the Conservative and Labour parties.

During the early part of the nineteenth century numerous influences combined to strengthen the connection between Scotland and England. Increased trade, improved communications, constant coming and going across the border and movement of population, intermarriage, loyalty to the same monarch, common victories, common sacrifices in a common cause, the influence achieved by individual Scots in every field of British life and, in return, the gradual spread to Scotland of English ideas and fashions and habits, all tended to break down the barriers which divided the two peoples. While it certainly could not be said that Scotland had been assimilated to England or vice versa, many of the old differences between them were beginning to disappear.

Already Scotland was a very different place from what it had been at the time of the Union. 'There is', wrote Sir Walter Scott in 1814, 'no European nation, which, within the course of half-a-century or a little more, has undergone so complete a change as the Kingdom of Scotland.' And as the nineteenth century

In 1888 crofters of the island of Lewis rioted against the inequities of the tenancy laws and land distribution. Sheriff Fraser of Stornoway, supported by Marines and police, reads the Riot Act. Many similar outbreaks of this time led to a Commission of Inquiry, and changes in the law.

The Forth Bridge, woven in silk by
Thomas Stevens of Coventry.

Leith Harbour from the Pier: water-
colour by T. H. Shepherd, 1829.

Dunbar fishing port, Haddingtonshire,
1882.

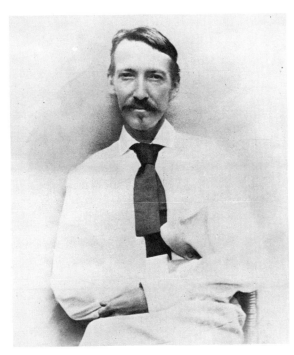

Robert Louis Stevenson.

progressed this became truer than ever. In the Highlands, in particular, the Gaelic language was, thanks to English but more still to Lowland Scottish influence, fast dying out, the number of native Gaelic speakers dropping from more than 250,000 in 1891 to 95,000 in 1951.

Equally, though Sir Walter's own influence continued long after his death to manifest itself in baronial castles and romantic novels and ballads, there were in Scotland no signs of any fresh national revival in the arts or in literature, comparable to that earlier flowering. Individual Scots, it is true, made names for themselves. In literature, Carlyle and Stevenson. In the arts, a handful of competent painters, Sir John Watson Gordon, a painstaking follower of Raeburn, Sir James Guthrie, the founder of the Glasgow school, McTaggart, MacWhirter and others. In architecture, 'Greek' Thomson, who adorned Victorian Glasgow with tenements and shops, merchants' offices and Presbyterian churches, all in a spirit of the purest classicism; Robert Lorimer, who stuck conscientiously to the historical, not to say baronial manner; and Charles Rennie Macintosh, whose vigorous originality and skilful use of traditional themes in a functional context won him a bigger reputation in Europe than in his own country. But of a new Scottish renaissance there was no sign.

Nor were there, for a century or so, many signs of serious discontent with the Union or of a vigorous nationalist or separatist movement. It was not until

1853 that the first stirrings of a new Scottish nationalism manifested themselves in the foundation of a National Association for the Vindication of Scottish Rights. This attracted some little support. Well-attended meetings were held and we learn that by 1880 Home Rule was 'distinctly and loudly mentioned'. So much so that in 1885 the London Government once again thought it advisable to appoint a special Minister with the title of Secretary for Scotland to take charge of Scottish affairs.

But this did not satisfy the advocates of Home Rule, who continued to demand self-government. At one time or another both the Liberal and Labour Parties committed themselves to Home Rule for Scotland and during the next fifty years or so various Home Rule Bills and resolutions were introduced. But though launched with a wealth of good will and good intentions, they made little progress towards the statute book. In 1907, however, a modest move was made in the direction of autonomy, when a Scottish Committee of the House of Commons was set up in which Scottish Members could deal with Scottish Bills.

The outbreak of war in 1914 made Scotland's own problems seem less immediate and for the next four years Scottish soldiers, sailors and airmen fought

Hunger marchers of the great depression. Scottish contingent in the march of protest against the Means Test, passing through Croughton, Northamptonshire, on 22nd October 1932.

bravely on all fronts for Great Britain and also for the concept of a British Empire so largely built by Scots. During these four years some seventy-four thousand Scotsmen gave their lives, a heavy toll for so small a country, as the War Memorials in every town and village in Scotland testify.

The peace and the economic depression that followed it brought a wave of disillusionment. Scotland, too dependent on heavy industry and textiles, both now suffering from severe foreign competition, was harder hit than England and suffered even worse unemployment. At the height of the slump in 1931 as many as 65 per cent of the shipyard workers on the Clyde were unemployed. Agriculture, too, was depressed. The result was widespread suffering and demoralization on a scale which was to deprive Scotland of some of the best elements in the country and to lead in the long run to dangerous and continuing depopulation. In Scotland it was widely felt that these misfortunes were due to London's neglect of Scotland's interests and the result was a revival of the Home Rule Movement. It was, in the words of Sir Robert Horne, 'the natural outcome of the sense of defeatism and humiliation engendered in the depression'.

London's answer was to promote the Scottish Secretary to be a Secretary of State with Cabinet rank and wider powers. This was in 1928. In 1939 these powers were further extended, when the functions in Scotland of the Departments for Home Affairs, Health, Agriculture and Education were vested in him. In the same year the headquarters of his Department were moved to St Andrew's House in Edinburgh, leaving only a small subsidiary staff in London. In 1951 provision was made for a Minister of State who was to act as deputy to the Secretary of State and to be based in Scotland. At the same time the number of Parliamentary Under-Secretaries of State was raised to three, each with specific functions.

In these ways Scotland achieved an ever greater measure of administrative independence. But the aim of the Nationalists was political independence. In 1934 two nationalist groups had merged to form the Scottish National Party. Five years later the Second World War broke out and the National Party's aspirations were temporarily eclipsed. Once more Scotland bore her full share of Britain's burden and once more tens of thousands of Scotsmen gave their lives in the common cause.

Though he was to be defeated at the General Election a few weeks later, the return to Parliament for the first time of a Scottish Nationalist candidate in April 1945 showed that Scottish Nationalism was not dead. The vast increase in the central power of the State (and therefore of London) caused by the war and fostered by the Labour Government of 1945 was bound to provoke a reaction in Scotland. However soothing it might sound to some English ears, the Socialist assertion that the 'gentleman from Whitehall knows best' had a far less reassuring ring north of the Border. In 1948 the scope of the Scottish Standing Committee was somewhat extended. But in the same year a fresh wave of Scottish Nationalist feeling culminated in the launching of a Scottish Covenant, calling for a Scottish Parliament within the framework of the United Kingdom, to which hundreds of thousands of signatures were appended all over Scotland. In 1950 the successful removal by the Nationalists of the Stone of Scone to Scotland from Westminster Abbey aroused grudging admiration even in England. And two years later the next reign was heralded all over Scotland by the merry crack of exploding pillar-boxes in protest against the new Royal Cypher, ERII, held by many to be insulting to Scotland.

For a time rather less was now heard of the Scottish National Party. But there was still an undercurrent of feeling in Scotland that insufficient attention was paid to Scottish affairs in Whitehall and that Scottish interests would be better served by increased devolution. This feeling was reinforced by the fact that ever since the war the unemployment figures for Scotland, under Labour and Conservative Governments alike, though better than between the wars, had even so run at approximately double the level for the United Kingdom.

The newest Covenant in Scottish history: in 1950 over a million and a quarter Scots signed this Covenant demanding a measure of self-government for Scotland.

The demand was reinforced – and still is – by the traditional graffiti.

The Labour victories of 1964 and 1966 and the consequent return to Socialist policies and increased centralization engendered as usual a strong recrudescence of Scottish national feeling and led in 1967 to the overwhelming victory at a by-election in the Labour stronghold of Hamilton of a Scottish Nationalist candidate, who, while the Union Jack was publicly burned by her supporters, declared amid scenes of enthusiasm that it was her aim to see Scotland seated at the United Nations between Saudi Arabia and Senegal. Though it was argued at the time that this was no more than a protest vote, it was a protest vote on a scale which made a powerful and in some ways salutary impact on the whole political scene and gave the old-established political parties serious food for

Mrs Ewing, the newly elected Scottish Nationalist M.P. for Hamilton, leaving to take her seat in the House of Commons, 16th November 1967.

Orrin Dam, in Glen Orrin, where a new loch has been formed as part of the Conon Valley development.

thought. Soon a variety of committees and commissions were busily enquiring into the advisability of a further measure of devolution for Scotland.

Once again, economic grievances and a feeling that Scotland was not getting a fair deal had contributed to this reaction and it was freely claimed by the Nationalists that Scotland would enjoy greater prosperity as an independent State than as part of the United Kingdom. This in spite of much evidence to the contrary and a world-wide trend towards larger, rather than smaller, economic units.

But the problem was not purely economic. Great Britain was passing at this time through a difficult period in her history, a period of change and frustration and disquiet. And this was reflected in a mood of growing disillusionment with politics and politicians. The issues of the day were neither clear-cut nor readily

Cruachan Dam, on Ben Cruachan. Water is pumped up 1,200 feet to the reservoir from Loch Awe.

comprehensible and to some people there seemed little to choose between the big London-based political parties. It was to this section of the electorate in particular that the simple, easily grasped slogan 'Scotland for the Scots' made an immediate and powerful appeal. It caught the imagination and aroused the emotions, which was all that it was required to do. Its precise implications could always be worked out later, though to most Scots the idea of an independent but diminished Scotland solemnly taking her seat at the United Nations 'between Saudi Arabia and Senegal' had as yet no great appeal.

Finally, the factor which, a hundred years earlier, had done as much as anything to make the Union acceptable to Scotland was now absent. In the century and a half that had followed the Union, Great Britain had become the heart of a great and expanding Empire, an Empire to which its citizens, whatever

their race, were proud to belong, an Empire that offered unlimited opportunities for men of parts, opportunities of which the Scots had taken their full share. Now this was no longer so. Britain had become a small country with big problems and a waning confidence in its own ability to solve them, a country which, as a distinguished American somewhat acidly observed, had 'lost an Empire and not yet found a role'. It was not so much that the Scots had suddenly discovered that they loved their own country more or took more pride in it. It was simply that some of them now took less pride than formerly in belonging to Great Britain, that the Union Flag no longer had quite the same meaning for them as in the days when so many of them had willingly died for it. Whether or

The New Forth Bridge, North Queensferry. With a span of 3,300 feet between the main piers, it is the largest suspension bridge in Europe.

not this particular mood persisted, would largely depend on Great Britain's ability to recover her old self-confidence and find her place in the modern world, and so rekindle in the Scots (and for that matter in the English) the wider patriotism of former years.

In Scotland, meanwhile, there was much that was hopeful. At times during the past half-century it had seemed as though recovery was too much to expect and there had been a tendency to take refuge in self-pity and despair. Now, despite the prevailing prophecies of doom, there emerged in Scotland in the early sixties undoubted indications of a breakthrough on the economic front, signs of reviving confidence and of new industries at long last coming to replace the old ones on which Scotland's former prosperity had been founded, of a trend away from narrow-based heavy industry and towards new, more widely diversified light industries and science-based industries. Living conditions, too, were better than they had ever been before. Agricultural production was on the increase. All of which went to prove, if proof were needed, that a better deal for Scotland depended not so much on constitutional adjustments (though they might help) but on a concerted effort on the part of all concerned and, first and foremost, on the part of the Scots themselves.

Meanwhile, quite apart from the more vocal manifestations of the Scottish National Party, a re-awakened national consciousness existed throughout the country, at all levels of society, strong enough to ensure that, come what might, Scotland, at any rate, would not succumb to drab, stereotyped uniformity, but would always keep her own natural character and uphold with undiminished vigour her own rights and interests as a nation.

Strachur, Argyll

Her Majesty the Queen, accompanied by the Duke of Edinburgh and Princess Anne, at the General Assembly of the Church of Scotland, 22nd May 1969.

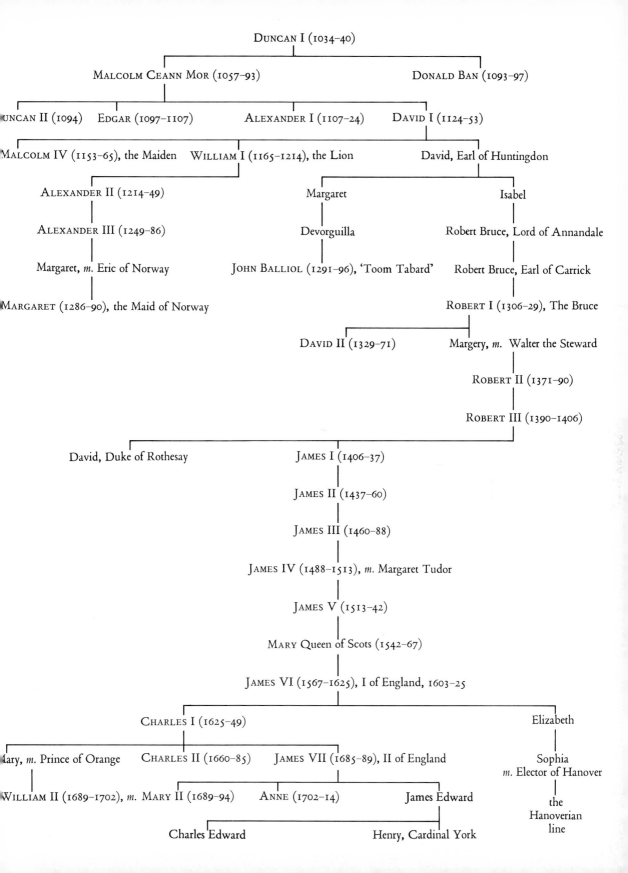

DUNCAN I (1034–40)

MALCOLM CEANN MOR (1057–93)   DONALD BAN (1093–97)

DUNCAN II (1094)   EDGAR (1097–1107)   ALEXANDER I (1107–24)   DAVID I (1124–53)

MALCOLM IV (1153–65), the Maiden   WILLIAM I (1165–1214), the Lion   David, Earl of Huntingdon

ALEXANDER II (1214–49)   Margaret   Isabel

ALEXANDER III (1249–86)   Devorguilla   Robert Bruce, Lord of Annandale

Margaret, m. Eric of Norway   JOHN BALLIOL (1291–96), 'Toom Tabard'   Robert Bruce, Earl of Carrick

MARGARET (1286–90), the Maid of Norway   ROBERT I (1306–29), The Bruce

DAVID II (1329–71)   Margery, m. Walter the Steward

ROBERT II (1371–90)

ROBERT III (1390–1406)

David, Duke of Rothesay   JAMES I (1406–37)

JAMES II (1437–60)

JAMES III (1460–88)

JAMES IV (1488–1513), m. Margaret Tudor

JAMES V (1513–42)

MARY Queen of Scots (1542–67)

JAMES VI (1567–1625), I of England, 1603–25

CHARLES I (1625–49)   Elizabeth

Mary, m. Prince of Orange   CHARLES II (1660–85)   JAMES VII (1685–89), II of England   Sophia
m. Elector of Hanover

WILLIAM II (1689–1702), m. MARY II (1689–94)   ANNE (1702–14)   James Edward   the
Hanoverian
line

Charles Edward   Henry, Cardinal York

List of Illustrations

Frontispiece 'From the Border to the Tay', detail of a map of Scotland, *c.* 1460. From Chronicle of England, by John Hardyng, a spy for Edward IV. *Bodleian Library, Oxford*, MS. Arch Selden B. 10, f. 184r.

8 Map of Scotland

9 Prehistoric standing stones of Stenness, Orkney. Crown copyright, reproduced by permission of the Ministry of Public Building and Works. *Photo Edwin Smith.*

Interior of house, Skara Brae, Orkney. Late Stone Age. Crown copyright, reproduced by permission of the Ministry of Public Building and Works. *Photo Edwin Smith.*

10 Gold Aureus of Hadrian. Bibliothèque Nationale, Paris. *Photo J. Roubier.*

11 Hadrian's Wall, completed *c.* AD 127. *Photo J. Allan Cash.*

12 Roman cavalryman and four northern tribesmen, armed with shields, swords and spears. Carved panel, detail of the Bridgeness slab from the Antonine Wall, 2nd century AD. *National Museum of Antiquities of Scotland, Edinburgh.*

13 Flagon, bowl and chalices. Roman silver, end of 4th century AD. Part of the Traprain Treasure, buried shortly after 400. *National Museum of Antiquities of Scotland, Edinburgh.*

14 Jet necklace from Poltalloch, Argyll. Middle Bronze Age. National Museum of Antiquities of Scotland, Edinburgh. *Photo Malcolm Murray.*

15 Hunting scene, relief from cross slab, Hilton of Cadboll, Ross-shire. Pictish, style of *c.* 800. *National Museum of Antiquities of Scotland, Edinburgh.*

Torrs chamfrain, unique Celtic bronze mask, possibly as early as 200 BC. Horns are also Celtic, added at a later date, making a false reconstruction. National Museum of Antiquities of Scotland, Edinburgh. *Photo Malcolm Murray.*

16 Papil Stone, found at an early ecclesiastical site on the island of Burra, Shetland. Pictish, early 9th century. *Crown copyright, reproduced by permission of the Ministry of Public Building and Works, Edinburgh.*

Aberlemno cross slab. Early Pictish sculptured cross, 8th century. *Crown copyright, reproduced by permission of the Ministry of Public Building and Works, Edinburgh.*

17 St Ninian. From Hours of Ninian, 15th-century Scottish manuscript. *Edinburgh University Library*, MS. 42, f. 72v.

18 St Columba, founder of Iona. Pen drawing from Adamnan's Life of St Columba, 9th century. *Stiftsbibliothek, St Gallen, Switzerland*, MS. 555, f. 166.

Iona Cathedral, with St Martin's Cross, Argyllshire. *Photo The British Travel Association.*

19 St Martin's Cross, Iona, Argyllshire. Free-standing cross of Irish type, probably 10th century. *Photo The Iona Community.*

Temptation of Christ, from the Book of Kells. By permission of the Board of Trinity College, Dublin. *Trinity College Library*, f. 202v.

20 St Mark, from the Book of Deer. Manuscript written in Latin, 9th century, with Gaelic additions, not shown, of the 11th century. From the Monastery of Deer, Buchan, Aberdeenshire, founded by SS. Columba and Drostan. *Cambridge University Library*, Ii. VI. 32, f. 16b.

Detail of Ruthwell Cross, Ruthwell Church, Dumfriesshire. Late 7th or early 8th century. Copy of the poem inscribed on the cross appeared in a 10th-century Italian manuscript. *Photo Edwin Smith.*

21 Viking sword hilt, from Eigg. Bronze, plated and inlaid with silver, $7\frac{1}{2}$ inches long, 9th century. National Museum of Antiquities of Scotland, Edinburgh. *Photo Tom Scott.*

22 Monymusk Reliquary in the shape of an early Irish church, 8th century. *National Museum of Antiquities of Scotland, Edinburgh.*

Hunterston Brooch, found near Largs, Argyllshire. Celtic, 8th century. *National Museum of Antiquities of Scotland, Edinburgh.*

23 Walrus ivory chessmen, from island of Lewis. Probably Scandinavian, 12th century. By courtesy of the Trustees of the British Museum. *Photo Edwin Smith.*

24 St Margaret, Queen of Scotland. Illumination from 15th-century manuscript, possibly written at Bourges for a Scottish lady. *By courtesy of the Trustees of the British Museum*, MS. Add. 39761, f. 93b.

25 Abernethy Round Tower, Perthshire.

Crown copyright, reproduced by permission of the Ministry of Public Building and Works, Edinburgh.

26 Charter of Duncan II, 1094, granting land of Tynninghame, Auldhame and other parts of East Lothian to the Abbey of St Cuthbert at Durham. *Reproduced by permission of the Dean and Chapter of Durham Cathedral.*

Tomb of the Kings, Iona, Argyllshire. *Photo Miss Diana Ashcroft.*

27 Panel from St Andrews sarcophagus shrine, St Andrews, Fife. First half of the 10th century. *Crown copyright, reproduced by permission of the Ministry of Public Building and Works, Edinburgh.*

28 Doorway from the cloister garth to the nave, Dryburgh Abbey, Berwickshire. *Photo Edwin Smith.*

29 Coin of David I, 1124–53. Sterling, first Scottish mint from Berwick. *National Museum of Antiquities of Scotland, Edinburgh.*

30 David I and Malcolm IV. Miniature from the Charter of Kelso Abbey, 1159. By kind permission of the Duke of Roxburghe. *On loan to the National Library of Scotland, Edinburgh.*

31 Coin of William I, 1165–1214. *National Museum of Antiquities of Scotland, Edinburgh.*

32 Coin of Alexander II, 1214–49. Sterling from Berwick. *National Museum of Antiquities of Scotland, Edinburgh.*

33 Viking silver penny from Birka, Sweden, c. 880. *By courtesy of the Trustees of the British Museum.*

Viking ship, detail from Sparlosa runic stone, Västergötland, Sweden, c. 800. *Photo Antikvarisk Topografiska Arkivet, Stockholm.*

A Parliament of Edward I in 1274. Print published in 1724. British Museum.

34 Detail of projected treaty of marriage between Maid of Norway and Edward I's son, 1290. *Crown copyright, reproduced by permission of the Controller of H.M. Stationery Office. Public Record Office, London, E. 36, vol. 274, Liber A., f. 188.*

35 Coin of John Balliol, 1292–96. Sterling, obverse. *National Museum of Antiquities of Scotland, Edinburgh.*

36 Detail of the 'Ragman's Roll', 28th August 1296. *Crown copyright, reproduced by permission of the Controller of H.M. Stationery Office. Public Record Office, London, C. 47/23/5.*

37 Letter from Sir William Wallace and Sir Andrew de Moray to the Mayors and Communes of Lübeck and Hamburg, 1297. *Archiv der Hansestadt Lübeck.*

38 Great Seal of Robert Bruce. *By courtesy of the Trustees of the British Museum, MS. Colt, Ch. XIX, f. 4r.*

39 Equestrian statue of Robert Bruce, Bannockburn, Stirling. *Photo The British Travel Association.*

40 Coin of Robert Bruce, 1306–29. Sterling, obverse. *National Museum of Antiquities of Scotland, Edinburgh.*

41 Air view of Caerlaverock Castle, Dumfriesshire. *Photo Aerofilms Limited.*

42 Battle of Bannockburn, 1314. Drawing from Scotichronicon by John Fordun, 15th century. Reproduced by permission of the Masters and Fellows of Corpus Christi College, Cambridge. *Corpus Christi College Library, MS. 171, f. 265.*

43 'The Arbroath Declaration', letter of the barons to Pope John XXII, 6th April 1320, with seals of barons. *Scottish Record Office, Edinburgh. Crown copyright,* reproduced by permission of the Controller of H.M. Stationery Office.

44 Cast of the skull of Robert Bruce. *Scottish National Portrait Gallery, Edinburgh.*

45 Bruce sword, inscribed with initials of Bruce, 'KRB', and Douglas, 'ILD', with instructions to Douglas to bury Bruce's heart in the Holy City. Dated 1320. Disputed authenticity. By kind permission of Rt Hon. Sir Alec Douglas-Home, Douglas Castle.

46 Perth besieged by the Earl of Mar, *c.* 1332. Woodcut from Holinshed's *Chronicles*, vol. I, 1577. British Museum.

47 Edward III with his prisoner David II, captured at Neville's Cross, 1346. Illumination from a 14th-century manuscript. *By courtesy of the Trustees of the British Museum, MS. Nero D, VI, f. 61v.*

Scots and French attack Wark Castle, Northumberland. Illumination from Froissart's *Chronicles*, 15th-century French manuscript. *By courtesy of the Trustees of the British Museum, MS. 18 E. 1, vol. II, f. 345.*

48 Coin of Robert II, 1371–90. Groat, obverse. *National Museum of Antiquities of Scotland, Edinburgh.*

49 The Cavers Standard of the Douglas family. *National Museum of Antiquities of Scotland, Edinburgh.*

50 Hermitage Castle, Roxburghshire. *Photo Edwin Smith.*

51 Cross of Ranald, son of John, Lord of the Isles, shown wearing a quilted warcoat, Celtic conical helmet, armed with claymore and battleaxe. *National Museum of Antiquities of Scotland, Edinburgh.*

Targe of Macdonalds, with double-headed eagle, the cognizance of the Lords of the Isles. Late 17th century.

223

National Museum of Antiquities of Scotland, Edinburgh. *Photo Tom Scott.*

Targe of Macdonald of Keppoch. Made of fir or oak boards, Celtic-type ornamentation, 18th century. *By courtesy of the Royal Scottish Museum, Edinburgh.*

52 Duart Castle, Mull. By kind permission of Sir Charles Maclean, Bt. *Photo The Scout Association.*

Maclean of Coll, sculptured tomb slab from Iona. From *Antiquities of Iona,* H. D. Graham, London, 1850.

53 View of St Andrews. Engraving from *Theatrum Scotiae,* John Slezer, 1693.

Mace of the Faculty of Arts, 1418. *By permission of the Librarian, St Andrews University.*

54 Parliament of James I in Edinburgh, 1424. Woodcut from Holinshed's *Chronicles,* vol. I, 1577. British Museum.

55 Aeneas Sylvius at the Court of James I. Fresco, 1505, by Pinturicchio. Siena Cathedral. *Photo Mansell Collection.*

57 Armorial bearings and inscription from tomb of James, seventh Earl of Douglas, St Bride's Chapel, Douglas, Lanarkshire. From *The Douglas Book,* W. Fraser, London, 1885. British Museum.

58 James II. Illumination by Jörg von Ehingen. *Landesbibliothek, Stuttgart,* Cod. Hist. 4°, 141.

59 Ecclesiastical seal of Bishop Kennedy of St Andrews, *c.* 1450. *Scottish Record Office, Edinburgh. Crown copyright, reproduced by permission of the Controller of H.M. Stationery Office.*

View of Inverness. Engraving from *Theatrum Scotiae,* John Slezer, 1693.

60 Portrait of James III. Detail from altarpiece, ascribed to Hugo van der Goes,

1476. *Reproduced by gracious permission of Her Majesty the Queen.*

61 Portrait of Margaret of Denmark, wife of James III. Detail from altarpiece ascribed to Hugo van der Goes, 1476. *Reproduced by gracious permission of Her Majesty the Queen.*

Coin of James III, obverse, probably earliest Renaissance-type portrait outside Italy, *c.* 1485. *National Museum of Antiquities of Scotland, Edinburgh.*

Coin of James III. Reverse, showing three pellets with an annulet, crown and fleur-de-lys in angles of cross. *National Museum of Antiquities of Scotland, Edinburgh.*

62 Battle of Sauchieburn, 1488. From *The Pictorial History of Scotland,* James Taylor, vol. II, London, 1859.

64 Portrait, called James IV. Flemish school, 16th century. *National Gallery of Scotland, Edinburgh.*

65 'Queen Mary's Harp', *c.* 1500. *National Museum of Antiquities of Scotland, Edinburgh.*

Palace of Linlithgow. From *Theatrum Scotiae,* John Slezer, 1693.

66 Andrew Myllar's printing device. *Reproduced by permission of the Trustees of the National Library of Scotland, Edinburgh.* F.7, d.27, p. 168.

67 Tomb of Alasdair Crotach, seventh Macleod Chief, St Clement's Church, Isle of Harris. Made in 1528. *Photo Edwin Smith.*

69 Map of the clans in the 16th century. From *The Highland Clans* by Sir Iain Moncreiffe of that Ilk, Barrie & Rockliff, 1967, by courtesy of the author and publishers.

71 Three merchants. 16th-century stone carving. *Courtesy of the Merchants' House, Glasgow.*

72 Model of the *Great Michael. By courtesy of the Royal Scottish Museum, Edinburgh.*

73 Portrait of Margaret Tudor, by Daniel Mytens. *Reproduced by gracious permission of Her Majesty the Queen.*

74 Signature of James IV from his letter to Henry VIII, 11 June(?) 1509. *By courtesy of the Trustees of the British Museum,* MS. Vespasian F. III, f. 77.

75 Standard of the Earl Marischal of Scotland, carried at the Battle of Flodden Field by Black John Skirving of Plewlandhill, the Earl's standard-bearer. 4 feet 7 inches long. *By courtesy of the Faculty of Advocates, Edinburgh.*

76 Portrait of Margaret Tudor and the Duke of Albany, Anonymous. By kind permission of the Marquess of Bute, Rothesay. *Photo Scottish National Portrait Gallery, Edinburgh.*

77 View of Stirling Castle. Engraving from *Theatrum Scotiae,* John Slezer, 1693.

78 View of the Palace of Falkland. Engraving from *Theatrum Scotiae,* John Slezer, 1693.

79 Portrait of James V and Marie de Guise-Lorraine, Anonymous. *Courtesy the Treasury, The National Trust, Hardwick Hall.*

Portrait of Marie de Guise-Lorraine, wife of James V, attributed to Corneille de Lyon. *Scottish National Portrait Gallery, Edinburgh.*

81 The Watson Mazer, mid 16th century. *By courtesy of the Royal Scottish Museum, Edinburgh.*

83 Title-page of the Geneva, or 'Breeches' Bible. British Museum.

84 Portrait of George Wishart, Anonymous. *University of Glasgow Art Collections.*

85 Portrait of John Knox, by Hondius, after the Beze, *Icones* version of 1580 from a painted portrait. British Museum.

86 George Wishart being burnt at the stake, St Andrews, March 1546. Woodcut from Holinshed's *Chronicles,* vol. I, London, 1577. British Museum.

Letter from Edward VI to the Duke of Somerset, 18th September 1547. *By courtesy of the Trustees of the British Museum,* MS. Lansdowne 1236, f. 16.

87 Plan of the Battle of Pinkie, woodcut from *The Expedicion into Scotlade of the Duke of Soomerset,* William Patten, 1548. British Museum.

88 *The Preaching of Knox before the Lords of the Congregation, 10th June 1559.* By Sir David Wilkie, 1832. *By courtesy of the Trustees of the Tate Gallery.*

89 Bands of the Lords of the Congregation, 1557. Reproduced by permission of the Society of Antiquaries of Scotland. *On loan to the National Library of Scotland, Edinburgh.*

90 Letter of John Knox to Mary Queen of Scots, originally written in 1556. Title-page from copy of Knox's *Historie of the Reformation of the Church of Scotland,* 1644.

91 Death of Henri II of France, 1559. Engraving by J. Tortorel and J. Perrissin. British Museum.

92 John Knox and 'Goodman' blowing trumpets against 'the Monstrous Regiment of Women'. Mary Queen of Scots is represented. From *An Oration against the unlawfull Insurrections . . . ,* Peter Frarinus, Antwerp, 1566. British Museum.

93 Page from *The First Booke of Discipline*, 1560, printed 1621. British Museum.

94 Frontispiece to 'Tennowr' part of the First Psalm. From *The Scottish Psalter* by the Reformer, Thomas Wode, Vicar of St Andrews, 1566. Possibly for use in the Chapel Royal, Holyroodhouse. *Edinburgh University Library.*

95 The 'Deuil Blanc' portrait of Mary Queen of Scots, probably painted in 1559 by François Clouet. *Scottish National Portrait Gallery, Edinburgh.*

96 Portrait of Henry Stewart, Lord Darnley, detail of painting by Hans Eworth. *Reproduced by gracious permission of Her Majesty the Queen.*

The Murder of Riccio, by Sir William Allan, 1833. *National Gallery of Scotland, Edinburgh.*

97 Plan of Kirk o' Field, 1567, showing the murder of Darnley. Contemporary drawing. *Crown copyright, reproduced by permission of the Controller of H.M. Stationery Office. Public Record Office, London,* SP 52/12, No. 1.

Miniature of James Hepburn, fourth Earl of Bothwell, 1566, Anonymous. *Scottish National Portrait Gallery, Edinburgh.*

Miniature of Mary Queen of Scots, Anonymous. By kind permission of the Duke of Portland, K.G., Welbeck Woodhouse. *Photo Victoria and Albert Museum.*

98 Battle of Carberry Hill, 1567. Contemporary drawing. *Crown copyright, reproduced by permission of the Controller of H.M. Stationery Office. Public Record Office, London,* SP 52/13, No. 58.

99 Writing and signatures of Mary Queen of Scots. From the Missal given to Mary by the Dauphin of France before their marriage, and used by her during the Fotheringhay imprisonment. Hermitage Museum, St Petersburg. *Photo Novosti Press Agency.*

100 Siege of Edinburgh Castle, 1573. Woodcut from Holinshed's *Chronicles*, vol. II, London, 1577. British Museum.

101 Portrait of George Buchanan, 1506, Anonymous. *Scottish National Portrait Gallery, Edinburgh.*

Portrait of James Stewart, Earl of Moray, Regent to James VI. Copy by H. Munro after an unknown artist. *Scottish National Portrait Gallery, Edinburgh.*

Portrait of James Douglas, fourth Earl of Morton, Regent to James VI, by Arnold Bronkhorst. *Scottish National Portrait Gallery, Edinburgh.*

102 Portrait of James VI and I as a boy, by Arnold Bronkhorst. *Scottish National Portrait Gallery, Edinburgh.*

104 Central panel from Oxburgh Hangings, silk on canvas, worked by Mary during her imprisonment. *Victoria and Albert Museum.*

Pen and ink sketch of the arrangements made for the execution of Mary Queen of Scots, at Fotheringhay Castle, 8th February 1587. *By courtesy of the Trustees of the British Museum,* MS. Add. 48027.

105 Portrait of James VI and I, and Anne of Denmark. Probably engraved soon after James's accession to the English throne, by Renold Elstrack. British Museum.

106 Title-page of the Gaelic translation by John Carswell of Calvin's *Catechism*, printed by Wreittoun, Edinburgh, 1631. *Reproduced by permission of the Trustees of the National Library of Scotland, Edinburgh.*

107 Triumphal arch for the entry of James VI and I into London. Engraving by Stephen Harrison, 1604. British Museum.

108 The coronation of James VI and I and Anne in Westminster Abbey, 25th July 1603. Contemporary engraving. British Museum.

109 Page from *Regiam Majestatem, The Auld Lawes and Constitutions of Scotland* by Sir John Skene. Printed by Thomas Finlayson, Edinburgh, 1609. British Museum.

111 Portrait of James VI and I, 1610, school of Marcus Gheeraerts the Younger, now attributed to J. de Critz. *By courtesy of the Trustees of the National Maritime Museum, Greenwich.*

113 Charles I at Edinburgh. Engraving by Cornelius van Dalen, probably executed in 1638. British Museum.

114 Title-page of the Book of Common Prayer for the Church of Scotland. Printed in Edinburgh, 1637. British Museum.

The 'Arch-Prelate' of St Andrews assaulted while reading the new Revised Prayer Book for Scotland imposed on the Scottish Kirk by Charles. Scene in St Giles's, Edinburgh, 1637. Etching by Wenceslaus Hollar for *Sight of the Transactions of these latter yeares*, John Vicars, 1646. British Museum.

115 Portrait of Alexander Henderson of Leuchars. Engraving by S. Freeman after the original. From *History of Scotland*, vol. III, George Buchanan, Glasgow, 1855. British Museum.

Portrait of James Guthrie of Stirling. Engraving by S. Freeman after the original. From *History of Scotland*, vol.

IV, George Buchanan, Glasgow, 1855. British Museum.

117 Signatures of Montrose and Earl of Rothes, from the National Covenant, 28th February 1638. *Edinburgh Corporation Museums, Huntly House.*

National Covenant, 28th February 1638, showing reverse side of the original document. *Edinburgh Corporation Museums, Huntly House.*

118 Portrait of James Graham, first Marquess of Montrose, after original by George Jamesone. By kind permission of the Earl of Southesk. *Photo Scottish National Portrait Gallery, Edinburgh.*

119 Portrait of Archibald Campbell, first Marquess of Argyll, Anonymous. *Scottish National Portrait Gallery, Edinburgh.*

121 The Government of Charles I. Contemporary engraving.

123 A Solemn League and Covenant for Reformation, as published in London, 25th September 1643. Top left panel illustrates English nobles, gentry and clergy solemnly taking the Covenant. Engraving by Wenceslaus Hollar.

Unfinished miniature of Oliver Cromwell, 1650's, by Samuel Cooper. By kind permission of the Duke of Buccleuch and Queensberry, K.T., G.C.V.O., Bowhill, Selkirk. *Photo National Portrait Gallery.*

124 View of Aberdeen Old College. Engraving from *Theatrum Scotiae*, John Slezer, 1693.

126–7 Battle of Naseby, 1645. Engraving from *Anglia Rediviva*, Joshua Sprigge, 1647. British Museum.

129 Execution of Charles I, January 1649. Contemporary German engraving. British Museum.

131 Crowning of Charles II at Scone, 1st January 1651. British Museum.

132 'Old Sayings and Predictions Verified and fulfilled Touching the Young King of Scotland and his gued subjects', broadside of 1651. British Museum.

133 House of Commons, reverse of the Great Seal of England. Appended to Oliver Cromwell's grant to Edward Horseman, dated Westminster, 8th September 1656. *By courtesy of the Trustees of the British Museum*, MS. Sloane 3243.

134 Portrait of Charles II, by Pieter van der Banck. Drawing, with false signature. *Reproduced by gracious permission of Her Majesty the Queen.*

135 View of Parliament House and the Exchequer. Engraving by Parr after Elphinstone. *British Museum, Department of Maps*, Kings XLIX, no. 68 E.7.

136 Silver quaich, engraved with thistles and tulips. Made by James Penman, Edinburgh, 1685. *By courtesy of the Royal Scottish Museum, Edinburgh.*
Murder of Archbishop Sharp of St Andrews, 3rd May 1679. Print published in London, 1679. British Museum.

137 Battle of Drumclog, 1st June 1679. Engraving by C. E. Wagstaff after original by George Harvey. British Museum.

138 Portrait of James VII and II, 1685–89, by Sir Peter Lely. *Scottish National Portrait Gallery, Edinburgh.*
Signatures of Charles II and his brother James, 1662. *By permission of the Royal Society.*

139 Signature of Graham of Claverhouse, Viscount Dundee, from his letter to the Earl of Linlithgow, Commander-in-Chief of Scotland. Glasgow, 1st June 1679. *By courtesy of the Trustees of the British Museum*, MS. Stowe 142, f. 95.

140 Scottish Dragoon of 1680. From *History of the Scottish Regiments in the British Army*, Alexander K. Murray, Glasgow, 1862. British Museum.

141 View of Dunkeld. Engraving from *Theatrum Scotiae*, John Slezer, 1693.
View of Dunfermline. Engraving from *Theatrum Scotiae*, John Slezer, 1693.

142 Siege of Londonderry, 1689. Engraving by Schoonebeck. *Photo Mansell Collection.*

143 Portrait of John Campbell, first Earl of Breadalbane, by Sir John Medina. *Scottish National Portrait Gallery, Edinburgh.*

144 Portrait of Captain Robert Campbell of Glenlyon, Anonymous. *Scottish National Portrait Gallery, Edinburgh.*

145 Duncanson's order for the massacre of the Clan Macdonald at Glencoe. Sent to Captain Robert Campbell, 12th February 1692. *Reproduced by permission of the Trustees of the National Library of Scotland, Edinburgh.*

146 Glencoe, Argyllshire. *Photo Edwin Smith.*

147 Highland Chieftain of the 1660's, by Joseph Michael Wright. *Scottish National Portrait Gallery, Edinburgh.*

148 Map of Darien. From 'A letter giving a description of Darien by an unknown person' sent to the Marquess of Tweeddale, 1699. British Museum.

149 Letter from Colin Campbell to his brother, 22nd December 1698. *Reproduced by permission of the Trustees of the National Library of Scotland, Edinburgh.*

151 Birth of Prince James Edward, 1688. Contemporary engraving. British Museum.

153 Portrait of John Campbell, second

Duke of Argyll, General of the Hanoverian troops during the 1715 Rising, by William Aikman. *Scottish National Portrait Gallery, Edinburgh.*

154 Signatures and seals of the Treaty of Union, 22nd July 1706. *Scottish Record Office, Edinburgh. Crown copyright, reproduced by permission of the Controller of H.M. Stationery Office.*

155 Duke of Queensberry presenting the Treaty of Union to Queen Anne. Anonymous engraving. British Museum.

156 The Crown of Scotland. *Crown copyright, reproduced by permission of the Controller of H.M. Stationery Office.*

159 Portrait of Prince James Francis Edward, 1701, by François de Troy. *Scottish National Portrait Gallery, Edinburgh.*

160–1 View of Perth. Engraving from *Theatrum Scotiae*, John Slezer, 1693.

162 Highland dirks, swords and targe, 17th and 18th centuries. *By courtesy of the Royal Scottish Museum, Edinburgh.*

163 Claymore, double-handed sword. Early example of its kind, possibly 16th century. *National Museum of Antiquities of Scotland, Edinburgh.*

164 Landing of Prince James Edward at Peterhead, January 1716. Line engraving by Peter Schenk. *Scottish National Portrait Gallery, Edinburgh.*

Execution of Jacobite Lords, Tower Hill, 1716. Anonymous line engraving. *Scottish National Portrait Gallery, Edinburgh.*

165 The captured rebels returning to London, 1715. Engraving by H. Terasson after L. du Guernier. British Museum.

166 *Fort Augustus*, by Paul Sandby. Pen and grey wash. *Reproduced by gracious permission of Her Majesty the Queen.*

167 General Wade's bridge, Aberfeldy, Perthshire. *Photo Edwin Smith.*

168 *The Porteous Mob.* Scene in Grassmarket, Edinburgh, 1736, with Captain Porteous being carried to dyer's pole on left. Painting by James Drummond, 1855. *National Gallery of Scotland, Edinburgh.*

169 Portrait of Prince Charles Edward, 1732, by Antonio David. *Scottish National Portrait Gallery, Edinburgh.*

170 Antoine Walsh taking leave of Prince Charles on shores of Loch nan Uamh, 1745. Contemporary drawing. *Scottish National Portrait Gallery, Edinburgh.*

171 Jacobite toasting glasses, 18th century. *Victoria and Albert Museum, London.*

172 *Entry of Prince Charles and Highlanders into Edinburgh after the Battle of Prestonpans.* Engraving by Frederick Bacon after original by Thomas Duncan. British Museum.

173 *A Race from Preston Pans to Berwick.* Print published 22nd September 1745. British Museum.

174 Portrait of Lord George Murray, Anonymous. By kind permission of the Duke of Atholl. *On loan to the Scottish National Portrait Gallery, Edinburgh.*

175 *The March to Finchley.* Engraving by William Hogarth, first published December 1750. *Photo Courtauld Institute of Art.*

176 French commanding officer surrendering the key of Carlisle to the Duke of Cumberland, 30th December 1745. Mezzotint by Miller after original by Thomas Hudson. British Museum.

177 *Tandem Triumphans*, Battle of Culloden, 16th April 1746. Anonymous engraving, published 7th May 1746. British Museum.

178 Cottage on the site of the Culloden battlefield. *Photo Edwin Smith.*

179 *Rebell Gratitude.* Anonymous engraving, published 14th January 1747.

180 Portrait of Flora Macdonald, after Allan Ramsay. *Scottish National Portrait Gallery, Edinburgh.*

The Agreable Contrast. Engraving by W. Ebersley, 1746. British Museum.

181 Portrait of William Augustus, Duke of Cumberland, by Sir Joshua Reynolds. *Scottish National Portrait Gallery, Edinburgh.*

182 Simon, Lord Lovat, appearing on trial before Lord Hardwicke, Lord High Steward, 1746. Engraving of 1791, after original by William Hogarth, sketched at the trial. British Museum.

183 Execution of rebel Lords at Tower Hill, 1746. Contemporary French engraving. British Museum.

184 Signature of **Charles Edward**, *c.* 1773, from a letter to Monsieur Nicolas Verzura, his banker in Paris. *Reproduced by permission of the Trustees of the National Library of Scotland, Edinburgh, MS. 593, no. 2033.*

185 Monument to the last three members of the House of Stuart, designed by Canova. St Peter's, Rome. *Photo Mansell Collection.*

186 *The General Assembly of the Kirk of Scotland,* 1787. Drawing by David Allan, known as the 'Scottish Hogarth'. *British Museum, Department of Maps, Kings XLIX, no. 68.g.2.*

187 Portrait of George IV, by Sir David Wilkie. *Reproduced by gracious permission of Her Majesty the Queen.*

188 *Queen Victoria landing at Loch Muich,* by Sir Edwin Landseer. Sketch, *c.* 1850, for original oil. *Reproduced by gracious permission of Her Majesty the Queen.*

189 *Edinburgh Castle, c.* 1750, by Paul Sandby. *Reproduced by courtesy of the Trustees of the Tate Gallery.*

190 Power-loom Weaving. Engraving from *History of Cotton Manufacture in Great Britain,* Edward Baines, London, 1835. British Museum.

Weighing the bar-lead, by David Allan. By kind permission of Sir James Hunter Blair, Bt, Maybole, Ayrshire. *Photo National Gallery of Scotland, Edinburgh.*

191 James Watt and the steam-engine, 1860. Engraving by James Scott after James E. Lauder. *Photo Science Museum.*

Opening of the Glasgow and Garnkirk Railway, 1831. Lithograph by W. Day. *Photo Science Museum.*

192 *Charlotte Dundas,* 1804. From *A Sketch of the origin and progress of Steam Navigation,* Bennet Woodcroft, London, 1848. British Museum.

P.S. *Comet,* 1812. Contemporary lithograph. *Photo Science Museum.*

Women grinding corn and 'walking the cloth'. Engraving from *Tour in Scotland,* vol. 1, Thomas Pennant, London, 1774–6. British Museum.

193 Eviction of tenants. Engraving from *Real Scottish Grievances,* Donald Ross, Glasgow, 1854. *Mitchell Library, Glasgow.*

194–5 View of Glasgow from the Necropolis. *Photo Edwin Smith.*

197 Portrait of Henry Dundas, first Viscount Melville, by Sir Thomas Lawrence. *National Portrait Gallery, London.*

198 *The Giant Factotum amusing himself,* by James Gillray, published 21st January 1797. British Museum.

199 Thomas Muir at his trial for sedition, 30th–31st August 1793. Engraving by I. Kay from *The Trial of Thomas Muir, Esq.*, Edinburgh, 1793, 2nd edition. British Museum.

200 Interior of the Academy of Fine Arts, University of Glasgow. Founded by the Foulis Brothers, fifteen years prior to the Royal Academy, London. Closed 1775 due to lack of funds. Etching by David Allan, *c.* 1760. British Museum.

Portrait medallion of David Hume, by James Tassie. *Scottish National Portrait Gallery, Edinburgh.*

Self-portrait, 1776, by Allan Ramsay. Red chalk drawing. *National Portrait Gallery, London.*

201 Interior of Laurieston House, Carlton Place, Glasgow. *Photo Edwin Smith.*

202 *Walter Scott with his friends*, by Thomas Faed. *Scottish National Portrait Gallery, Edinburgh.*

203 Portrait of Robert Burns, 1787, by Alexander Nasmyth. *Scottish National Portrait Gallery, Edinburgh.*

Colonel Alastair Macdonell of Glengarry, Chief of Macdonells, by Sir Henry Raeburn. *National Gallery of Scotland, Edinburgh.*

206 Portrait of James Keir Hardie, by C. Rowe. Pencil sketch. *National Portrait Gallery, London.*

207 Reading the Riot Act at Aignish Farm, near Stornoway. From *Illustrated London News*, 21st January 1888. *Photo Radio Times Hulton Picture Library.*

208 The Forth Bridge, a Stevengraph. By kind permission of Sir Arthur Elton, Bt, London.

Leith Harbour from the Pier, 1829, by Thomas H. Shepherd.

Dunbar fishing port, Haddingtonshire, 1822. Engraving by William Daniell.

209 Portrait of Robert Louis Stevenson. *Edinburgh Corporation Museums, Lady Stair's House, Lawnmarket.*

210 Unemployment march to London, 22nd October 1932. *Photo Radio Times Hulton Picture Library.*

212 Scottish Covenant of 1950. *Photo Radio Times Hulton Picture Library.*

213 Home Rule for Scotland graffito. *Photo Radio Times Hulton Picture Library.*

Mrs Winifred Ewing, Scottish Nationalist Party M.P., elected 1967. *Photo courtesy of S.N.P. Headquarters, Edinburgh.*

214 Orrin Dam. *By courtesy of the North of Scotland Hydro-Electric Board.*

215 Cruachan Dam, on Ben Cruachan. *By courtesy of the North of Scotland Hydro-Electric Board.*

216–17 New Forth Bridge, North Queensferry. *Photo Edwin Smith.*

218 Queen Elizabeth at the General Assembly of the Church of Scotland, 22nd May 1969. *Photo Press Association.*

Index

Page numbers in italics refer to pictures

Aberdeen, 29, 52, 124; King's College, 66
Abernethy, 25
Act of Classes, the, 129, 131
Act of Revocation, 112
Act of Security, 151, 155, 157
Act of Settlement (1701), 151
Adam brothers, 200
Aeneas Sylvius, 55–6
Agricola, Cnaeus Julius, 10
agriculture, 192, 211, 218
Aidan, Saint, 20
Aidan the False, 19
Alban (early name for Scotland), 15, 20
Albany, Duke of (son of Robert II), 49, 50
Albany, Alexander, 3rd Duke of, 61, 62
Albany, Charlotte, Duchess of, 184
Albany, John, 4th Duke of, 76
Albany, Murdoch, 2nd Duke of, 54
Alberoni, Cardinal, 166
Albert, Prince, 188
Alexander I, 26
Alexander II, 32
Alexander III, 32–4
Aliens Act (1705), 152
Alnwick, Northumberland, 25, 31
American Civil War, 190
American War of Independence, 189, 199

Angles, 20, 22
Anglo-Saxons, *see* Saxons
Angus, Archibald Douglas, Earl of ('Bell-the-Cat'), 61–2
Angus, Archibald Douglas, 6th Earl of, 75–6, 77
Angus Og, 40
Angus Og (son of John Macdonald of the Isles), 68, 70
Anne, Queen, 150, 152
Anne of Denmark, 105
Antonine Wall, 10, 11, *12*
Applecross, 20
Arbroath Declaration, the, 43–4
Argyll, Archibald, 5th Earl of, *89*, 92
Argyll, Archibald, 8th Earl of, 119, 120, 122, 125, 129; and Charles II, 130; support for Commonwealth, 133; execution, 134
Argyll, Archibald, 9th Earl of, 139
Argyll, Colin Campbell, 1st Earl of, 62
Argyll, John Campbell, 2nd Duke of, 152, 157, 163, 164, 168, 184
Arkinholm, Battle of, 60
Arran, James, 1st Earl of, 76, 79, 88
Auld Alliance, the, 31, 55, 73, 93
Ayala, Pedro de, 63, 65, 70

Bailleul, Bernard de, 27
Balliol, Edward, 45–6
Balliol, John ('Toom Tabard'), 35–6
Balloch of Islay, Donald, 55
Bannockburn, Battle of, 41, *42*, 43
Barrie, Sir James, 204
Barton, Sir Andrew, 72
Beaton, Cardinal David, 79, 83–4; assassination of, 86–7
Beaton, James, Archbishop of St Andrews, 84
Beaufort, Lady Joan, 54, 56
Bede, the Venerable, 20
Belhaven, John Hamilton, 2nd Lord, 154
Berwick, 36, 43, 46, 48, 62, 119; Treaty of, 93; Pacification of, 120
Bible, translation of the, 82
Bill of Pains and Penalties (1736), 168
Birgham, Treaty of, 34
bishops and bishoprics, 29, 30, 105, 106, 110
Bishops' Wars, the, 120
Black Agnes, 47
Black Watch, the, 167, 169
Blair, Robert, 133
Blind Harry, 65
Bloody Bay, Battle of the, 70
Book of Common Order, The (Knox), 93, 107
Border raids, 49, 51

Bothwell, 1st Earl of, 63
Bothwell, James, 4th Earl of, 97, 98
Bothwell Brig, 137
Boulogne, Treaty of, 87–8
Boyd, Mary, 81
Boyd, Robert, Lord, 61
Braxfield, Robert Macqueen, Lord, 199
Breadalbane, John Campbell, 1st Earl of ('Iain Glas'), 142
Brechin, 29
Bruce, Robert, the Elder, 35, 36
Bruce, Robert, the Younger (later Robert I), 38–40; victory at Bannockburn, 41–3; and the Church, 41, 43–4; recognized as King, 44; death of, 44–5
Brus, Robert de, 27
Buchan, son of Regent Albany, 52, 53
Buchanan, George, 101
Buckingham, George Villiers, 1st Duke of, 112
burgh status, 29, 196
Burns, Robert, 200, 201, 203
Burt, Lieut. Edward, 68
Bute, 47, 196

Caithness, 16, 21, 29, 32
Calgacus, 10, 183
Cambuskenneth, 45
Cameron, Clan, 171, 178, 183
Cameron, Richard, 137, 139
Cameronians, the, 139
Cameron of Lochiel, Donald, 171
Campbell, Colin, 204
Campbell of Glenlyon, Captain Robert, 144, 147
Campbells of Argyll, the, 110
canals, 191
Candida Casa, 16
Carberry Hill, 98
Carbisdale, 130
Cardross, 44
Carham, Battle of, 22
Carlyle, Thomas, 209
Caroline, Queen, 168
Castletown, 160

Cecil, Sir Robert, 103, 104, 107
Celestine III, Pope, 31
celibacy, 24
Celts, 14–15, 20–1
Chalmers, Thomas, 204
Charles I, 112, 113 ff.; and the liturgy, 113, 115–16; Parliamentary opposition to, 119–20; civil war, 120 ff.; execution, 129
Charles II, 130; Scottish campaign, 130–2; coronation at Scone, 131; and the Covenanters, 134–7
Charles VII of France, 55
Charles Edward 169, 171 ff.; as 'King over the water', 184; see also Forty-Five
Charlotte Dundas, the, 192
Chattan, Clan, 178
Chevy Chase, 49
Christianity, coming of, 15–16, 19–20
Church, the early, 19, 20–1; under David I, 29, 30; relations with English Church, 31; corruption under Mary Queen of Scots, 81–2, 94; under James V, 82
Church of Scotland, the, 94, 105, 112; austerity in, 94–5; and the Covenant, 122; patronage in, 204; see also General Assembly
Civil War, the, 120 ff.
clan system, the, 66–8, 69, 109–10, 193
Clearances, the, 193
Clement V, Pope, 43
Clydeside, 190–1, 211
coinage, see mints
Colquoun of Stobo, Adam, 81
Columba, Saint, 18, 19, 22
Comet, the, 192
Committee of Articles, 56, 109, 120, 135
Committee of the Estates, 132
Company of Scotland Trading to Africa and the Indies, the, 147–8, 152
Comyn, Red John, 36, 38;

murder of, 39
Confession of Fayth, The (Knox), 93
conventicles, 136
Cope, Sir John, 171, 172
Corryarick, Pass of, 171
cotton industry, the, 190, 206
Covenant, the National, 116, 118–19, 122, 130; see also First Covenant
Covenanters, 136–7
Craigmillar, 65
Cramond, 11
Cranmer, Archbishop, 89
Crawford, David Lindsay, 4th Earl of ('Earl Beardie'), 58, 60
Crichton, Sir William, 57, 58
Cromwell, Oliver, 123, 128, 129, 130, 133
Culloden, Battle of, 176–9
cultural and intellectual life, 65, 200–3
Cumberland, William Augustus, Duke of, 174, 176, 177, 178, 181
Cumbernauld, 122
Cunninghame Graham, R.B., 206
Cuthbert, Saint, 20

Dalriada, Kingdom of, 15, 16, 18–19, 20
Dalrymple, Sir John, see Stair
Darien, 147 ff.
Darnley, Henry Stewart, Lord, 96–7
David I, 26, 27–30
David II, 44, 45, 46–8, 50
Davidson, Sir Robert, 52
Defoe, Daniel, 157
depression, economic, 211
Derwentwater, James Radcliffe, 3rd Earl, 162
Disarming Act (1746), 182, 197
Divine Right of Kings, 112
Donald Ban, 25, 26
Douglas, 4th Earl of, 51, 53
Douglas, Archibald, 5th Earl of, 55, 56
Douglas, Archibald, 46
Douglas, Gavin, 65

Douglas, James, 7th Earl of, 57, 58 n.
Douglas, James, 9th Earl of, 60
Douglas, Sir James, (the Black Douglas), 40, 45, 50
Douglas, William, 6th Earl of, 57
Douglas, William, 8th Earl of, 58
Douglases, the Black, 49, 50–1, 57–60
Douglases, the Red, 61, 76, 80
Dreux, Yolette de, 34
Dryburgh Abbey, 28, 29
Dumbarton Rock, 88
Dumfries, 39, 41; in the Forty-Five, 175
Dunadd, 18, 21
Dunbar, William, 65, 81
Dunbar Castle, 47
Dunblane, 29
Duncan I, 22–3
Duncan II, 28
Dundee, 41, 125, 132
Dundee, Viscount, see Graham of Claverhouse
Dunkeld, 22
Dunstaffnage, 41
Dupplin Moor, Battle of, 46

'Earl Beardie', 58, 60
Ecgfrith, King, 21
Edgar, son of Malcolm III, 26
Edgar the Atheling, 23, 25
Edinburgh, 41, 47, 162, 168, 189, 205; Castle, 57, 61; 'Cleanse the Causeway', 76; early printing in, 66; sacked by Henry VIII, 80; Treaty of, 93; St Giles's Cathedral, 113
Edward I of England, 33, 34–6, 40
Edward II of England, 34, 40–1, 44
Edward III of England, 44, 45, 46, 47, 48
Edward IV of England, 68
Edward VI of England, 79, 88, 89
Elcho, David, Lord (later 2nd Earl of Wemyss), 124

Elcho, David, Lord (later 5th Earl of Wemyss), 175, 179
Elizabeth I of England, 91–2, 98, 103, 107
Elizabeth II, Queen, 189
emigration, 193
Engagement, the, 128
Eochaid the Venomous, 19
episcopacy, 24, 105
Episcopal Church, the, 204–5
Erasmus, Desiderius, 63
Eric II of Norway, 33
Ettrick Shepherd, the, 203
Eugenius IV, Pope, 81

Falaise, Treaty of, 31, 32
Falkirk, Battle of, 38
Falkland Palace, 65, 78
Fergus, Prince of Galloway, 32
Fergus of Dalriada, 36
feudal system of ownership, 27, 30
'Fifteen', the, 160 ff.
First Blast of the Trumpet, The (Knox), 92
First Book of Discipline, The (Knox), 93
First Covenant, the, 89–90, 91
fitzAlan, Walter, 27
fitzAlan, Walter, Lord of Renfrew, 32
fitzAlan, Walter ('Walter the Steward'), 45
Five Articles, the, 110, 112
Flodden, Battle of, 74–5
Fontenoy, Battle of, 169
Forbes of Culloden, Duncan, 168, 176, 181
Forster, Thomas, 162
Fort Augustus, 167
Fort George, 167
Fort St Andrew, 149, 150
Fort William, 142, 167
'Forty-Five', the, 171 ff.
franchise system, defects of, 196; widening of, 206
François I of France (husband of Mary Queen of Scots), 90, 91–2
Fraser, Clan, 162–3, 172
Fraser, Rev. James, 130

Fraser, William, Bishop of St Andrews, 35
Fraser of Tweeddale, Sir Simon, 38, 40
Free Church of Scotland, 204
French Revolution, 199

Gaelic language, 27, 30, 63, 167, 209
Galloway, 32
Geddes, Jenny, 115
General Assembly, the, 94, 103, 106, 110, 112, 113, 181, 189; and the National Covenant, 118, 120; of 1842, 204
George I, 158
George III, 186
George IV, 186, 188
George VI, 189
Glasgow, 29, 31, 125, 189; in the Forty-Five, 175; modern growth of, 194
Glencoe, massacre of, 144–6
Glenfinnan, 171
Glenshiel, 166
Glentrool, 40
Gordon, Clan, 163
Gordon, Sir John Watson, 209
Gowrie, William, 3rd Earl of, 103
Graham of Claverhouse, John, 137, 139
Grampians, 11
Great Michael, the, 72
Guise, Marie de, 78, 79, 84, 87, 88; and John Knox, 89; and Protestantism, 92; death of, 93
Guthrie, Sir James, 209

Hadrian, Emperor, 10
Hadrian's Wall, 10, 11
Hakon, King of Norway, 32–3
Halidon Hill, Battle of, 46
Hamilton, James Hamilton, 1st Duke of, 116, 128
Hamilton, James Douglas, 4th Duke of, 153, 154, 156
Hamilton, Archbishop John, 88
Hamilton, Patrick, 83
Hanoverian Succession, 151–2, 158

Harlaw, 52
Hay, Archibald, 81
Hebrides, *see* Western Isles
Henderson of Leuchars,
　Alexander, 115, 116
Henry I of England, 30
Henry II of England, 31
Henry IV of England, 50, 51
Henry V of England, 53
Henry VI of England, 60
Henry VII of England, 73
Henry VIII of England, 73–4,
　75, 76, 77, 78, 79–80, 84, 86
Henryson, Robert, 65
Highland regiments, 193, 197;
　see also Black Watch,
　Cameronians
Holy Island, 20
Holy League, the, 73
Holyroodhouse, 96, 110, 115,
　189
Home, Sir Alexander, 1st Baron,
　62
Home, Alexander, 3rd Baron, 74
Home Rule, 207, 210, 211
Hope, Sir Thomas, 115
Hopeful Binning of Bo'ness, The,
　150
Horne, Sir Robert, 211
Hume, David, 200
Huntingdon Chronicle, The, 22
Huntly, George Gordon, 6th
　Earl of, 103

industry, 19th-century growth of,
　190–1
Innocent III, Pope, 29
Inveraray, 125, 143, 162
Inverkeithing, 131
Inverlochy, Battle of, 55
Inverness, 59, 70, 176; Castle,
　162
Iona, *18*, 19, 20, 22, 26; Statutes
　of, 110
Ireland, invasion from, 18
Isabel, Queen of England, 44
Isobel, Countess of Buchan, 40

Jacobites, 139, 142, 154, 157–8,
　166, 169, 170, 181; evictions

of, 183–4; *see also* the Fifteen,
　the Forty-five
James I, 50, 54–6
James II, 56, 58–60
James III, *60*, 61–2
James IV, 63, *64*, 68*ff.*, 74;
　policy towards the Highlands
　and Islands, 70–1; foreign
　policy of, 71–2; relations with
　England, 72–3
James V, *75*, 76*ff.*, 79, 82
James VI (I of England), 98,
　101, 103*ff.*; marriage, 105;
　religious views, 105, 108, 110;
　succession to English throne,
　103–4, 107; policy towards the
　Highlands, 109–10; death, 112
James VII (II of England),
　138–9, 143
James Edward (James VIII
　and III), 150, 157, 158, 160,
　164–5
Joan of Arc, 55
John XXII, Pope, 43
Johnson, Dr Samuel, 183
Journal of Our Life in the Highlands,
　188
justice, administration of, 29

Keir Hardie, James, 206
Kelso Abbey, 29
Kenmure, William Gordon,
　6th Viscount, 162
Kennedy, James, Bishop of St
　Andrews, 58, *59*, 61
Killiecrankie, Battle of, 139
Killing Time, the, 137
Kintyre, 26
Kirkwall, 33
Knox, Andrew, Bishop of the
　Isles, 110
Knox, John, 84, *85*, 87, *88*, 91,
　98; visit to Geneva, 89; and
　the 'rascal multitude', 92;
　formulation of creed and
　constitution, 93
'Knox's Liturgy', 93

Labour Party, 206–7, 210
Lambert, General, 131

Lanark, 37
Largs, Battle of, 33
Laud, William, Archbishop of
　Canterbury, 113, 120
Lauderdale, John Maitland, 2nd
　Earl of, 128, 134, 136
Lennox, Esmé Stewart, 1st Duke
　of, 101, 102
Leslie, Alexander, 119, 120
Leslie, David, 123, 130–2
Letters of Fire and Sword, 109
Liberal Party, 205–6, 210
Linlithgow Palace, 55, 65
Lismore, 20
Livingstone, David, 204
Lochleven Castle, 98
Loch Ness, 19
Lollius Urbicus, 10
Lord Advocate, 196, 198
Lords of the Congregation, *88*,
　89–90
Lords of Erection, 112
Lords of the Isles (Macdonald),
　32, 33, 51, 68, 110
Lords of Lorne (Macdougall),
　32, 41
Lorimer, Robert, 209
Lorne, Archibald, Lord
　(afterwards 9th Earl of Argyll),
　115
Loudon Hill, 40
Louis XIV of France, 158
Louis XV of France, 170
Lovat, Simon Fraser, Lord, 162,
　167, 175–6
Luther, Martin, 77

MacAlpin, Kenneth, 21, 22
Macbeth, 23
Macdonald, Clan, *51*, 162, 171,
　178
Macdonald of Boisdale, 171
MacDonald of Clanranald, 171
MacDonald of Glencoe,
　Alexander MacIan, 143–4,
　146
Macdonald of the Isles,
　Alexander, 55
Macdonald of the Isles, Donald,
　51–2
Macdonald of the Isles, Donald

Dubh, 70, 80
Macdonald of the Isles, John, 58, 60, 68, 70
Macdonald of Lochalsh, Alexander, 70
Macdonald of Moidart, 70
Macdonald of Sleat, 171
Macdonalds of Islay, 109
MacDonell of Glengarry, 143
MacErc, Fergus, Angus and Lorne, 18
MacGregor, Clan, 162
Mackay, Clan, 163, 175
Mackay, General Hugh, 139, 142
Mackenzie, Clan, 175
Mackintosh, Charles Rennie, 209
Mackintosh of Borlum, William, 162
Maclachlan, Clan, 179
Maclean, Clan, 52, 131, 142, 162, 163, 171, 179, 183
Maclean, Hector (Red Hector of the Battles), 52
Maclean of Ardgour, 70
Maclean of Duart, 70, 110, 163
Maclean of Duart, Hector, 131
Maclean of Drimnin, 179
Macleod, Clan, 67, 175
Madeline, wife of James V, 78
Maelbeatha, 23
Maelrubba, Saint, 20
Magnus III of Norway (Barelegs), 26
Magnus VI of Norway, 33
Maitland of Lethington, Sir Richard, 93
Malcolm II, 22
Malcolm III Ceann Mor, 23, 24-5
Malcolm IV ('the Maiden'), 30-1
Mar, Alexander Stewart, Earl of, 52
Mar, Donald, Earl of, 46
Mar, John, Earl of (son of James II), 61
Mar, John Erskine, 6th Earl of ('Bobbing John'), 158, 160-2, 163, 164

Margaret, Saint (wife of Malcolm III), 23, 24, 25
Margaret, Queen ('the Maid of Norway'), 34
Margaret (wife of Alexander III), 33
Margaret (daughter of Alexander III), 33
Margaret of Denmark, 61
Margaret Tudor (wife of James IV), 73, 75, 76
Margery (daughter of Robert I), 45
Marie de Guise, see Guise
Marlborough, John Churchill, 1st Duke of, 155
Marston Moor, Battle of, 123
martyrdom, 94
Mary, Queen of England, 89, 91
Mary Queen of Scots 79, 88, 95 ff.; marriage to Dauphin, 90-1; marriage to Darnley, 96; marriage to Bothwell, 97; abdication, 98; execution, 104
Maud (wife of Henry I of England), 26
Maud (daughter of Henry I of England), 30
Medici, Catherine de, 77
Melrose Abbey, 29
Melville, Andrew, 106, 110
Melville, Henry Dundas, 1st Viscount, 196, 197
mints and coinage, 29
missionaries, early Christian, 15-16, 19, 20
Moluag, Saint, 20
Monck, General George, 132, 133
Moncreiffe, Hill of, 10
Monmouth, James, Duke of, 137, 139
Mons Graupius, 10
Montrose, James Graham, 5th Earl of, 115, 118, 120, 122, 129; campaign for Charles I, 123-5; service to Charles II, 130; execution, 130
Moray, 26, 32
Moray, Sir Andrew de, 38
Moray, James Stewart, 2nd Earl of, 98, 101, 103

Moray, Thomas Randolph, Earl of, 45
Moray of Bothwell, Andrew, 46
Morel, 25
Mortimer, Roger, 1st Earl of March, 44
Morton, James, 4th Earl of, 89, 101-2
Muir, Thomas, 199
Mull, early churches on, 19
Munro, Clan, 163, 175
Murray, Lord George, 174, 175, 177
Myln, Walter, 90

Naseby, Battle of, 125, 126-7
nationalism, 209-10, 211
Navigation Act, 147
Nectansmere, Battle of, 21
Nesbit Muir, Battle of, 48
Neville's Cross, Battle of, 47
Ninian, Saint, 16, 17
Norman Conquest, the, 23, 24
Norman influence, 27, 29
Northampton, Treaty of, 44
Norway, Norsemen, 21, 22, 23, 26, 29, 32-3

Ogilvy, Sir Alexander, 52
Oran, Saint, 19
Orkneys, 9, 16, 21, 33, 61
Ossian, 200, 203
Otterburn, Battle of, 49

Palmer, Thomas, 199
Park, Mungo, 204
Parliament, Scottish, 45, 109, 120, 129, 132, 133, 135, 147, 151, 152, 155-6
Parliament, Westminster, 195-6, 198, 199, 205-6; and the Church, 204; Scottish Standing Committee, 210, 212
Paterson, William, 147-9
Perth, 41, 46, 47, 112, 124; taken in the Fifteen, 161; in the Forty-Five, 171
Picts, 14-15, 16, 19, 21, 22
Piggott, Sir Charles, 109

Pinkie Cleugh, Battle of, 80, *86*, 87
population figures, 194
Porteous, Captain, 168
Prayer Book, the, 113, 115, 118
Presbyterianism, 105, 110, 112, 123, 125, 128, 134, 157; unity of Scottish, 204
Prestonpans, Battle of, 172
Privy Council (Scottish), 109, 134, 135, 136, 152
Protestantism, 79, 80–1, 84, 88, 89–90, 92, 93, 107

Queensberry, James Douglas, 2nd Duke of, 153, 155, 156

Raeburn, Sir Henry, 200
'Ragman's Roll', the, 36
railways, 191–2
Ramsay, Allan, 200
Red Harlaw, the, 52
Reformation, the, 77–8, 92, 94
Reform Bill (1832), 205
Renaissance, the, 65
Riccio, David, 96
Richard I of England, 31
roads and road-building, 167, 191
Robert I, *see* Bruce
Robert II, 45, 47, *48*, 49
Robert III, 49
Roman occupation, 10–13
Ross, 26, 29
Ross, Clan, 163
Rothes, John Leslie, 6th Earl of, 115
Rothesay, David, Duke of (son of Robert III), 49
Rough Wooing, the, 80, 84
Rous, Francis, 123
Roxburgh, 41, 60
Ruthven, Raid of, 103

St Andrews University, 52, *53*
Sauchieburn, Battle of, 62, 63
Saxons, 13, 14
Scots, early, 15, 19, 21
Scott, Sir Walter, 188, 198, 200,

201, 203, 204, 207, 209
Scottish Miners' Federation, 206
Scottish National Party, 211, 212; representation at Westminster, 211, 213
Scrymgeour, Sir James, 52
Second Book of Discipline, The (Knox), 106
Secretary of State for Scotland, 134, 168, 195, 210, 211; Master of Stair, 142, 147
Sermoneta, Cardinal, 82
Severus, Emperor, 11
Sharp, James, Archbishop of St Andrews, 135, 137
sheep-farming, 193
Sheriffmuir, Battle of, 163
Shetland, 16, 21, 33, 61
shipbuilding, 190–1, 192, 211
Sibylla (wife of Alexander I), 26
Sinclair, Oliver, 78
Smith, Adam, 200
Solemn League and Covenant, 122, 123, 125, 130
Solway Moss, Battle of, 78
Somerled, Lord of Argyll, 31, 32
Somerset, Edward, 1st Duke of, 80, 87
Sophia of Hanover, Electress, 151
Spottiswoode, Archbishop John, 107, 110, 113
Squadrone Volante, 154
Stair, the Master of (Sir John Dalrymple, later Earl of Stair), 142, 143, 146, 152
Standard, Battle of the, 30
Statutes of Iona, 110
Stephen, King of England, 30
Stevenson, Robert Louis, 209
Stewart, Alexander, Archbishop of St Andrews, 74, 82
Stewart, Lord James, 92
Stewart, Robert, *see* Robert II
Stewart of the Orkneys, Patrick ('Earl Pate'), 109
Stirling, 10, 41, 47, 77; Castle, 59, 77, 88; in the Forty-Five, 176
Stirling Bridge, Battle of, 37
Stone of Scone, 36, 212
Strafford, Thomas Wentworth, Earl of, 120

Strathclyde, 14, 21, 23
Surrey, John, Earl of, 37
Sutherland, 16, 21
Sutherland, Clan, 163, 175
Sutherland clearances, the, 193

Tables, the, 115
Tacitus, Cornelius, 10
Tertullian, 16
Testament of Cresseid (Henryson), 65
Thistle and the Rose, The (Dunbar), 65
Thomson, Alexander, 209
Tippermuir, 124
Tiree, early churches on, 19
'Toom Tabard', *see* Balliol
trade, foreign, under David I, 29; with the Low Countries under James IV, 66; under William and Mary, 147
trade unions, 206
Traprain Law, 13
Trent, Council of, 88
Troyes, Treaty of, 53

Union, Act of (1607), 108
Union, Treaty of, 133; negotiations under Queen Anne, 152, 154; enactment of, 155–6; unpopularity of, 157, 158, 161, 166; eventual effects of, 189, 199
Union Jack, the, 108
United Free Church, 204
Utrecht, Treaty of, 158

Valence, Aymer de, Earl of Pembroke, 40
Victoria, Queen, 188

Wade, Field-Marshal George, 167, 173–4
Wallace, William, 37–8; poem by Blind Harry on, 65
Walpole, Horace, 175
Walpole, Sir Robert, 168
Walter the Steward, *see* fitzAlan

Warbeck, Perkin, 72
Warriston, Archibald Johnston, Lord, 115, 116
Watt, James, 191
weights and measures, standard system of, 29
Western Isles, the, 21, 26, 32, 33
Westminster-Ardtornish, Treaty of, 68

Westminster Confession of Faith, 123, 147
Whithorn, 16
Wilkie, Sir David, 200
William I ('the Lion'), 31
William I of England, 25
William of Orange, 139, 148; and the Highlanders, 143-6; and Church problems, 147

Wishart, George, 84, 86
Wood, Sir Michael, 72
Worcester, Battle of, 132
World War, First, 210-11
World War, Second, 211
worship, forms of, 107

York, Henry, Cardinal, 186